Shipping Smarter

SHIPPING SMARTER

A Guide to eCommerce Shipping

Steven Visic and Chris Madden

R^ethink

First published in Great Britain in 2021
by Rethink Press (www.rethinkpress.com)

Contents

Introduction

Many business owners start out with no knowledge of shipping and pretty much wing it, trying to learn along the way. There is no definitive knowledge base that guides them in understanding how to ship goods easily, profitably and correctly, ending up in much wasted time, money and pain. In many cases, failing at online shipping leads to loss of sales, damaged or lost product, excessive returns and bad customer reviews. Ultimately the merchant can end up as just another failed small business statistic.

We have spent the majority of our working lives in the Australian transport industry in a variety of roles from operations, to customer service, to sales and management with some of Australia's largest carriers. We are directors of Smart Send, Australia's longest-serving online courier aggregation company.

We have helped thousands of customers succeed with shipping and we have a special yearning to help start-ups and small businesses succeed when shipping their goods. It's a passion we hold to this day: to see a fledgling idea or product come to fruition and become a shipping success story. Similarly, we pride ourselves on our ability to assist an existing business struggling with overwhelming shipping problems and to see the day they come out the other side stronger and better than before.

Shipping Smarter shares our knowledge and expertise of this industry for any business that ships goods. What we've found over our combined forty-five-plus years in the transport industry is there are three main areas where most businesses encounter shipping problems:

- Pick-up issues
- Delivery problems
- Wasted time and unnecessary expense

In this book, we delve into the subsections of these three main areas. By the time you have finished reading *Shipping Smarter*, you will be able to remove many frustrations associated with shipping your products, enabling you to focus on initiatives to scale, grow and become a high-growth business.

Throughout this book, you will learn the fundamentals of shipping, key for establishing a solid platform from which you can propel your business. These include:

Sourcing products: If you're looking to start an eCommerce business or are sourcing new products to sell, our tips will help you make some vital and smart decisions.

Packaging: Your choice of packaging for your products is important to ensure damage and loss rates are minimised. It's vital to take the extra precautions when packaging your goods.

Reasonable and unreasonable expectations: Our experience and tips will help you understand what reasonable and unreasonable expectations are when shipping your products. The sooner you understand these, the sooner you start making smart shipping decisions.

Evolution of Australian carriers: We discuss the evolution of Australian carriers, so you understand where they've come from and where they're going.

Signature on delivery and authority to leave services: We consider what these terms mean and how to avoid the common pitfalls at delivery.

Shipping charges: How carriers calculate their shipping charges can vary greatly depending on factors such as location, product profile/packaging, weight/dimensions, speed of delivery and more. Understanding this will help you form smarter choices when shipping your products.

Cubic volume vs deadweight: You will get an understanding of the difference between these two charge weight calculation methods and how you may be able to save on shipping costs for your particular products based on their weight and size when shipped.

Surcharges: There are a multitude of potential surcharges you could incur when shipping – we'll discuss these extensively to help you minimise extra costs you may not have factored in.

International shipping: This can be a minefield. We'll help you understand what's involved in shipping globally from Australia and who the main players are.

We also discuss solutions and big picture thinking to allow you to set up a seamless, sustainable business by removing bottlenecks to do with shipping. We discuss topics such as:

- Website platforms to use for eCommerce. Some are better than others and we'll explain why. This alone can see a business thrive or dive.

- Technological solutions to streamline your shipping. If you want to become a scalable, profitable and high-growth business, utilising these are essential.

- What dropshipping and 3PL are, whether you need either solution to scale and which is best for your business.

- What marketplaces are and which, if any, you should consider.

- Partnering with trusted shipping partners and the reasons why price isn't the only factor to consider (or the most important). We've seen many businesses stagnate or die by partnering with the wrong shipping solution/carrier.

- By considering your shipping and delivery options beforehand, you will equip yourself with the knowledge and resources to succeed.

ONE
Starting An Online Store

In this chapter, we discuss:

* The growth of eCommerce
* Key trends
* Prompt eCommerce delivery, tracking and customer service
* The marketplace opportunities

The growing eCommerce wave

Online shopping is increasing faster than growth in traditional retail bricks and mortar businesses. More and more bricks and mortar businesses are augmenting online to increase their reach and stay connected with their customers.

In 2019, Australian online purchases saw a steady year on year growth of 17.2%. The year started strongly; however, there was a slump towards June 2019, with a similar trend in the second half of 2019 before slowing in anticipation of the Black Friday/Christmas sales. As expected, the busiest period of the year was the four weeks leading up to Christmas (including Black Friday and Cyber Monday). The highest growth areas were in the fashion/apparel and variety stores section which saw an online growth of 21.0% and 22.3% respectively.[1]

Data and statistics in Chapter One are sourced from Australia Post's annual eCommerce report, which highlights trends that should be considered by every online business.

Key trends

Sales events

Black Friday and Cyber Monday week (late November/early December) was the largest online shopping period

---

1   Australia Post, 'eCommerce update: Online sales continue to change the way we shop' (Australia Post, 2020), https://auspost. com.au/content/dam/auspost_corp/media/documents/ eCommerce-update.pdf, accessed 25 January 2021

for the second year running, growing 31.6% YOY in 2019.[2] It's worth noting, the change in timing of the event may have contributed to the increase.

Vogue Online Shopping Night (VOSN) in October, Amazon Prime Day in July and AfterYAY Day in August ran for extended periods in 2019 (in fact, double the length of those in 2018) and saw stronger growth compared to previous years.

Click Frenzy and May Mayhem slowed slightly but still placed in the top twelve shopping weeks for 2019, suggesting they still have a strong presence in the eCommerce calendar.

Black Friday and Cyber Monday grew 31.6% year on year in 2019.

What the above tells us is online shopping is here to stay. The 2020 COVID-19 pandemic has also changed the way we shop. Sales events are creating opportunities in many growth areas and are beginning to replace bricks and mortar retail. What critical factors have been unveiled?

---

2   Australia Post, 'eCommerce update: Online sales continue to change the way we shop' (Australia Post, 2020), https://auspost.com.au/content/dam/auspost_corp/media/documents/eCommerce-update.pdf, accessed 25 January 2021

Buying shifts in 2020

Major shopping events such as Black Friday and Cyber Monday are predicted to shift buyer behaviour.

Typically, the first half of the year is quieter than the second half, though COVID-19 in 2020 changed this with volumes exceeding those seen leading into Christmas 2019. This pandemic has altered the way many Australians shop (5.2 million households shopped online in April 2020 – an increase of 31% compared to the average in 2019), moving traditional shoppers online. Many believe the change will be permanent as shoppers experience the ease of shopping from home in their own time. This was reflected with Easter weekend 2020 being the biggest period in online shopping history. Online shopping was up by a massive 91% year on year in the week leading up to Mother's Day 2020.

Prompt eCommerce delivery, tracking and customer service

Speed of delivery matters

Next business day deliveries continued to grow above average in 2019, up 21.1% YOY.[3]

---

3   Ibid

Variety stores and health and beauty were the biggest adopters of next business day delivery in 2019, growing at 56.9% YOY.[4]

While fashion and apparel purchases accounted for over 59.8% of all next business day deliveries in 2019, growth softened to 11.5% YOY.[5]

As shoppers move more and more online, fast delivery services are an expectation, not an extra service which needs to be factored into your business plan.

Transparent tracking and customer service

Planning ahead for Christmas and other peak periods is vital to be prepared for the lift in volumes and the ever-increasing expectations of customers. They expect fast deliveries and seamless customer service. Buyers also expect transparent tracking, pre-alerts by SMS or emails, and they expect to be able to get all of this while they get on with their day-to-day lives.

The right delivery partner(s)

It is vital to the success of every eCommerce business that you understand and select the right delivery partners. From our experience, selecting a transport company is often an afterthought – more a necessary evil – but it really doesn't need to be like that. With

---

4   Ibid
5   Ibid

some homework, planning and understanding, you can get this vital piece of the puzzle right.

Throughout this book, we will explore how important it is you partner with the right delivery partner that reflects your branding and the image you wish to reflect to your buyer.

There is more to be considered when selecting your delivery partners than price alone. We'll take you through each step you need to take into account for you to have a greater understanding of the industry in general and have all the tools to get the vital delivery component of your business spot on.

Rakuten Advertising in their *APAC e-Commerce 2020 Report* found the top three reasons Australian shoppers chose a site to purchase from were:[6]

- Delivery times and updates – 56%

- Variety of products – 51%

- Cashback and rewards options – 38%

While the top three reasons for not completing an online purchase were:

- High shipping costs – 54%

---

6   Lalisa Fungtammasan, 'The Road to Recovery: 2020 e-Commerce in Asia-Pacific' [blog post], Rakuten Advertising Blog (16 September 2020), https://blog.rakutenadvertising.com/en-uk/insights/asia-pacific-eCommerce-2020, accessed 25 January 2021

- Long shipping wait time – 40%
- Difficulty returning items – 36%

This highlights the importance of having a smart shipping strategy and working with reputable partners.

Marketplace opportunities

The main benefit of utilising an online marketplace is they take care of the marketing and you gain access to a huge marketplace of buyers looking for similar products to yours. This alleviates the need for you to come up with your own marketing campaign which may hit or miss depending on your experience.

There are many marketplaces in Australia now with the main options being:

- eBay
- Amazon
- Etsy
- Catch.com.au
- Mydeal.com.au

There is a cost charged by the marketplaces ranging from a few percent up to 35% or more of your sale price. Your challenge is to weigh up the margin left over after paying seller fees and decide whether it's worthwhile (ie some products will be better suited to these marketplaces than others).

Due to eBay's longstanding presence and foothold in Australia, they continue to rule the pack with around seventy-four million visits per month and a 22% share (interestingly this isn't the case in the US where Amazon wins easily). eBay Plus is eBay's answer to Amazon Prime (which is a huge success overseas). By signing up to either programme and paying an annual fee, buyers receive benefits such as fast delivery, free delivery, discounts, online streaming services and much more. The main benefit for sellers is they receive improved or prioritised search results for their product listings which can mean more conversions and sales.

Amazon is a relative newcomer only starting in Australia in late 2017 but gaining momentum with around 2-3% share by mid-2019.[7] Similar to eBay, with Amazon you can sell on their platform and gain access to a huge base of customers (if you use Amazon's FBA service they can even store and ship sales orders for you). In a recent *Australian Financial*

7   Alex Wu, 'Not delivering: Amazon underperforming in Australian e-commerce' (IBISWorld, 2019), www.ibisworld.com/industry-insider/media/3606/enterprise_amazon_apr2019.pdf, accessed 25 January 2021

Review article, they estimate by 2029 sales to reach $23 billion in Australia.[8]

Etsy is the place to be if you're an artist or hobbyist. This marketplace attracts buyers looking for products in this segment or vintage products only. Catch.com. au (rebranded from Catch of the Day) and Mydeal. com.au are other up-and-coming marketplaces to consider. Large brands such as Nike, Adidas, Bonda and Yves Saint Laurent are flocking to both.

Why customer reviews are fundamental

Selling on marketplaces relies heavily on customer reviews. This is good in one way because it reinforces trust with buyers; however, it can also harm you or your brand. With Amazon, for example, there have been some horror stories where sellers have been banned for as little as three or four bad reviews with little recourse for dispute in Amazon's automated response system.

It is imperative to have a good policy in place for customer complaints facilitating lenient views on returns, damaged goods, change of mind, etc, or your business could feel the unfortunate wrath of the customer reviews process.

---

8   Sue Mitchell, 'Amazon Australia sales to reach $23b in 10 years' *Financial Review* (2019), https://www.afr.com/companies/retail/amazon-australia-sales-to-reach-23b-in-10-years-20191003-p52xfb, accessed 25 January 2021

Consider free shipping

eBay heavily pushes sellers to offer free shipping at checkout. This is great with speed at checkout for customers and is becoming an expectation from many consumers (particularly for small or lightweight goods).

Unless you're actually selling these smaller products (that can easily ship in satchels or small parcels at flat shipping rates across Australia), you may get stung badly when your courier provider charges you high country onforwarding charges for a delivery to a rural or remote area.

WHAT'S THE COST?

A number of years ago, we were approached by a potential new customer selling handbags and wallets successfully for years on eBay. His eBay listings promoted free shipping as one of his marketing points.

In the past few weeks, he had also begun selling large ornate tea chests. His newly found problem was with the free shipping he offered. He was receiving a high number of orders from regional or rural Australia as buyers in these locations often take advantage of free shipping offers online. The shipping costs to these areas was more than the cost of his product! He was losing money on every regional sale. We came up with a way to instead set a flat rate for shipping in his eBay listing for different regions of Australia which ultimately saved his bacon.

The moral of the story: Do your homework to ensure you're not going to lose out with your shipping strategy.

Marketplace tips from online merchants

We recently spoke to several online sellers about which sales or social platforms work best for them, and we were surprised by some of their replies.

eBay has been huge in Australia for the last twenty years, with social media playing a big part in their sales funnel. Facebook and Instagram enable sellers to target their desired market easier and accurately giving them a greater audience with marketing ROI improvements. Several we spoke to use Facebook and Instagram to point the buyer to their website to complete the purchase. It's clear that in today's marketplace you must have a multi-channel approach which includes social media.

The sellers we spoke to felt they had great success where they could tell a story that engaged their customers in a way that added more value to their products. One brand that has told brilliant stories to sell their products for many years is jpeterman.com – go to their website and read the outstanding stories written for each product.

If you're only using eBay or Amazon, the customers are not yours. eBay has also made changes recently to make it harder for you to get valuable customer data for your own business use. It is difficult – sometimes impossible – for you to gather valuable customer data required to build a successful brand off eBay.

Using a multi-channel approach not only gives you far more options to sell in many different places at the same time, but you also have more opportunities to market to your own customer base regularly. Selling via your own website also removes the costly marketplace seller fees, leaving you with more money in your own pocket.

It is clear that whatever your thinking, make sure you do your homework first to know which channels are going to work best for you.

TOP TIP: MULTI-CHANNEL MARKETING PAYS OFF

When retailers implement multi-channel marketing plans, customer retention increases by 91%. While there are many reasons for this, the largest is the fact that nine out of ten customers want cross-channel eCommerce, and they're willing to stick with the brands that offer it.[9]

---

9   M Lazar, 'These cross-channel eCommerce statistics prove it's the new normal' (Ready Cloud, 2019) www.readycloud.com/info/these-cross-channel-eCommerce-statistics-prove-its-the-new-normal, accessed 25 January 2021

Summary of key points

In this chapter, we learned:

- How eCommerce needs to be part of a growth strategy
- How buyer behaviour is shifting throughout the year
- How choosing the right delivery partners is key for maintaining speed and transparency with customers
- How customer reviews and engaging with multi-channel are fundamental to growing business and maintaining brand image

TWO

The Right Transport Partner For Your Brand

In this chapter, we discuss:

- How delivery providers can impact brand image

- The importance in having a variety of shipping options

- The different types of transport carriers and services available

- Using a courier company direct vs a courier aggregator

- Courier reviews

Your transport partner impacts your brand image

It is important to first explore who might be able to ship the products you're considering selling online. This is vital to the long-term success of your eCommerce store.

Pretty much anything can be shipped these days; it comes down to how much the product is worth and how easy the delivery can be. An example of this would be you're considering importing deck spas, which are large and heavy. If you don't know how you're getting these delivered to buyers or have an idea of how much this is likely to cost, then you're in trouble and may lose money getting the product delivered. But if your products are books, they can fit into a satchel or small carton and can be shipped easily and cheaply Australia-wide, meaning you can budget in a flat shipping rate or offer free shipping when you've done your homework. Does the transport company align to your brand? This is not often considered but is important. Paying bottom dollar may not be your best option; focusing on the attributes and strengths of transport partners is. After all they are a reflection and extension of your business. Choose wisely.

Consider this: you're in the business of selling high-end Hi-Fi equipment online. You want your buyers to feel they are getting their money's worth and feel they are valued from the time they purchase the goods up until delivery. You want them to feel the love.

Why would you risk sending with the cheapest possible transport supplier, when delivery is slow, and their customer service team is most likely based overseas? You want to give your customers a champagne service from purchase to delivery, so it makes sense to select a transport partner that reflects the same values as you. Your customer can have peace of mind that their high-end Hi-Fi equipment is in good hands and that it will arrive on time and intact. They can get excited and plan for the delivery. Happy with the process, they will leave you a great online review. Better still, confident you deliver what you say you do, they may place another order or refer their friends to your store.

HEAVY LIES THE CHAIR...

Years ago, we had a customer, Tony, who had a range of large massage chairs with a dead weight between 90 kg to 150 kg depending on the model. His problem came about because in his business plan, he had not explored the last mile shipping options and what was required before importing the chairs.

Tony really wanted to provide his buyers with a personalised delivery service where the chairs were delivered into the home, unpacked and installed. Unfortunately for Tony, this is not a service that most transport companies provide at a competitive price (or at all). What he needed was a furniture removalist company with two men who would ring the receiver beforehand to ensure they are available, turn up within the requested delivery window, unpack and install the chair and, more often than not, remove the packaging. This would have been perfect for Tony's needs and his brand, but the cost for this service was prohibitive and not factored into his original business plan.

What Tony could afford was a regular transport service, but this also came with pitfalls for Tony and his team. The chairs were oversized and too heavy for one person to handle, so he needed a tail-lift truck vehicle for every delivery which added more costs. If the delivery address had stairs, oftentimes the chairs – too heavy for the drivers – were left at the bottom of the stairs for the receiver to try and manhandle inside (as courier drivers are not required to enter the property). The list of problems went on.

All of this stress could have been avoided if Tony had investigated all the possible transport partners and the costs involved before finalising the importation of the massage chairs. He'd have known what he was up against before he had a warehouse full of massage chairs and no budget left to get them to the buyer.

He needed this information to brand his chairs as a premium offering to include the premium delivery service. If the research was in place prior to purchasing, Tony could have set himself apart from his competitors. There was scope for increased profits by marketing a premium massage chair and in-house delivery with the packaging removed for the buyer. This would have added value to his offering and allowed him to increase his prices for greater profitability.

The moral of the story: Make sure you explore and plan your shipping options before you import your items and start selling.

Your transport partners are one of the most important decisions you'll make for your online store. Selecting the right products and business model from the start is everything. If possible, we recommend the following:

- You should keep your packages under 30 kg dead weight. Flat pack furniture, for example, might include more than one package – if you can, try to keep each carton / flat pack under 30 kg when shipped.

- You should avoid sending anything over 150 cm (120 cm is best) in length.

- You should avoid sending fragile items (glass, porcelain and ceramics are not generally covered against damage in transit).

If you take this into consideration when sourcing your products, you're setting yourself up for success. You will also have many more shipping carriers and options available to you. The better you understand what easily can be handled by your transport partner and what can't, the fewer problems you'll have once they are on their way.

To recap, you need to take into account:

- What is the size and dead weight of each item?

- How is each item packaged (internally and externally) – will it arrive intact?

- Does the transport company align to your brand?

- How many transport companies are there that you can work with?

- What is the transport company's freight profile (they all have one)?

- When is a tail-lift truck service required?

- Are the items fragile? How could this impact you?

- If you already have a provider, does their freight profile match all your products?

- If you decide to sell fragile items, how many extras do we need to cover possible damages? Have you factored in a damage percentage to your business plan?

- Does the product contain batteries? Dangerous goods = extra costs and more paperwork.

Knowledge is power. With knowledge, you can make better decisions around your product lines and ship more successfully and cost effectively.

CAREFUL, IT'S FRAGILE

Ken, an old customer of ours, was sourcing glassware from China and the product was sent out from his

Sydney home to his Australian buyers in the same thin, single walled cardboard cartons in which he received the product from his Chinese supplier. As you can guess, this was a recipe for disaster. His damage rates were astronomical because the cardboard cartons were thin, single walled and regularly collapsed entirely in transit when another carton was placed on top in the carrier's trucks. The cartons simply weren't strong or robust enough to handle Australian courier/freight conditions.

The moral of the story: Make sure you have the right packaging for your fragile items.

When shipping any product – let alone fragile items – please ensure you not only have adequate internal packaging to protect the products, but also ensure the cartons used to ship the orders to your customers are double or triple walled cartons and brand new. This will provide the best possible support for the contents while in transit.

We have heard customers who end up with a damaged shipment say, 'The goods arrived fine in a 40-foot container all the way from China to Australia. Why was it damaged sending the carton interstate?' The simple fact is when goods move from China to Australia, they may be handled manually only three or four times from supplier to your door (ie placed into a container in China, unloaded from the container in Australia, loaded into a delivery vehicle in Australia and delivered to your door). When goods are sent domestically across Australia, they could be handled up to ten times or more in some situations.

An extreme example would be a carton sent via road freight from Cairns, Queensland to Margaret River, Western Australia could be handled manually twelve times: picked up from sender in Cairns, unloaded in local Cairns depot, reloaded in Cairns depot into linehaul vehicle, unloaded from linehaul vehicle in Brisbane, reloaded into another linehaul vehicle in Brisbane, unloaded from linehaul vehicle in Melbourne, reloaded into linehaul vehicle in Melbourne, unloaded from linehaul vehicle in Perth, reloaded into linehaul vehicle in Perth, unloaded from linehaul vehicle in Margaret River (or nearby town), reloaded into delivery vehicle and unloaded to receiver's door in Margaret River.

As you can see this item was handled three times more than a movement from a Chinese supplier to Australia. The important thing to remember is the more often an item is handled manually, the more chance it could be damaged in transit. To add to this, if your item is fragile, there is an even higher chance it could be damaged. To add further, imagine now sending the glassware in the customer story scenario above, the chances of it surviving and being delivered intact are even slimmer.

The other thing to consider is when goods travel in a 20-foot or 40-foot container from China, there is minimal movement within the container and usually all the products within the container are uniform, the same size/shape and packed tightly. In a road freight environment in Australia, hundreds or thousands of different sized products and items are shipped within the same linehaul or delivery vehicle – increasing the chance of a heavy, sharp or unusually shaped item being placed on top of, next to or falling onto your product. This reinforces our recommendations to ensure your product is well packaged when shipped to give it the best chance possible of arriving intact to your customer.

Brand alignment checklist

Depending on your brand and product's profile, carefully consider the right transport service. The table below represents a typical shipping service strategy by merchants.

Brand alignment checklist to avoid bad reviews

Product	Cheap road courier	Mid-range road courier	Premium express courier
Fidget spinners	✓	X	X
$30 sport shoes	✓	X	X
$250 sport shoes	X	✓	✓
$15 shorts	✓	X	X
$500 dress	X	X	✓
$300 bike	X	✓	X
Expensive jewellery	X	X	✓

In the examples above, the fidget spinners, $30 sport shoes and $15 shorts are low-cost items which means you most likely cannot afford to ship them via a mid-range or premium express courier service. You will have to make do with a cheap road courier service or Australia Post road option. Buyers aren't going to put up with paying high shipping costs which may be more than the value of their goods purchase.

Whereas the $250 sports shoes are most likely a well-known brand and expensive relative to their category, therefore, you should consider offering a mid-range road courier service and premium express service to your customer base as these services will be more in line with your product profile or brand. The customer can choose their preference with speed of delivery between the two services offered at checkout.

The $500 dress is an expensive fashion item and simply shouldn't be sent on a road service. You need to impress your high-end customer and provide premium express delivery services to match the transaction and get it to your customer quickly. As the dress can easily fit in a small courier satchel, you should be able to access flat rate pricing, and the more expensive price for delivery can be borne due to the high cost of the eCommerce transaction.

With the $300 bike, this is neither a cheap or expensive item relative to the category and, due to its size, the best fit would be a mid-range road courier option. You most likely could not afford to use a premium express courier option as the cost would be prohibitive.

As the expensive jewellery is a high-dollar value shipment and will also be a small package when sent, the obvious option would be an express courier for security, speed and brand alignment.

Variety in shipping options

As a seller, it's all about options and choice when it comes to shipping. Our business Smart Send began for this reason fifteen-plus years ago. There was little choice or many competitive shipping options for small and medium-sized enterprises (SMEs), and we began operations with a niche offering to this segment.

If you are currently utilising only one courier provider for your shipping or Australia Post, for example, it may pay to review your options (see sample table below). Each provider has strengths and weaknesses in different areas; some offer great pricing for light-weight/small items, others are great for mid-range products and others are best for shipping heavy products. This is also the case for levels of service: some providers are great delivering to capital cities where they use their own courier network but once the delivery address is in a rural or country area they struggle, have minimal online tracking capability or take much longer to deliver than other providers.

Comparing Australia Post and different couriers

	Competitive pricing (kg)				Size (cm)			Network coverage		
	0–5	6–22	23+	0–100	101–180	181+	Capitals	Rural	International
Australia Post	✓	✓	X	✓	X	X	✓	✓	✓
Courier A	X	✓	✓	✓	✓	X	✓	X	X
Courier B	✓	✓	X	✓	✓	✓	✓	✓	X
Courier C	X	X	✓	✓	✓	✓	✓	✓	✓

NB Australia Post information is correct as at year end 2020

SIGN ON DELIVERY

Matt sells memorabilia for $2,000 or more per piece. The high-dollar value means he requires a signature on delivery and transparent tracking. He was using one provider to ship nationally but found deteriorating levels of service (particularly with getting signatures for all his shipments and country deliveries were becoming an issue), resulting in more requests for refund from his customers.

Upon our suggestion, he settled on a courier company and Australia Post, with both providers servicing his needs. This meant he received improved shipping costs for his country deliveries and signature on delivery for all his shipments.

The moral of the story: Be sure you are using the best service(s) for your specific company needs.

Australia Post vs courier and freight companies

A regular question we get asked is: 'Should I use Australia Post or a courier company?' Each comes with benefits and weaknesses – ultimately, it comes down to your product profile, personal needs and your shipping strategy. SMEs need to consider the strengths and weaknesses of each option.[10]

---

10   Information is correct as at year end 2020

Australia Post

Strengths

- National network of Australia Post locations
- Competitive pricing for items up to 5 kg
- Online Application Programming Interface (API) to streamline shipping
- Handy range of packaging supplies
- Integration with eBay
- PO box and parcel locker delivery options

Weaknesses

- Can only transport items up to 100 cm
- Can only transport items up to 22 kg
- No pick-up service for low volume businesses
- No dangerous/hazardous goods carriage
- Not competitive for multiple item shipments
- Up to forty-eight hours response time to online service issue queries lodged via Australia Post site

Courier and freight companies

Strengths (varies by provider)

- Competitive pricing for a range of products

- Can transport products up to 1,000 kg per item
- Can transport items up to 6 metres
- Competitive options for multiple item shipments
- Pick-up from your door (some regional/rural areas excluded)
- Popshops and redelivery options

Weaknesses

- Cannot deliver to PO box, parcel lockers (only to street addresses)
- Not all provide national network of depots
- Must provide your own packaging
- Hidden surcharges can surprise you
- Varying levels of customer service should issues arise

Transport carriers and service types

If you're starting out or haven't researched the market much, there are different types of transport segments available:

- Road express (which encompasses courier and freight companies)
- Express premium national

- General and bulk carriers

- International carriers (air and sea freight)

- Local same day

- Taxi truck

- Post

- Furniture removalists

- Drones (stay tuned)

If you're in eCommerce, you may use a variety of these services depending on your product profile and shipping strategy.

Road express

From our experience this is the most common method of delivery for eCommerce stores. This type of service provides value for money as it is delivered fairly quickly nationally at a decent price. Road express carriers include companies like TNT Express, Star-Track Express, Couriers Please, Fastway/Aramex Couriers, Allied Express and many more. The range of products suitable for road express can vary from 500 grams to 1 tonne. All products must be suitably packaged for shipment.

Express premium national

This service was previously called 'air express' as most of the deliveries are delivered nationally with use of an aeroplane. Many years ago some shipping companies ran into legal issues with the name 'air express' because some customers complained that nearby deliveries (eg shipping from Sydney to Melbourne) ended up travelling via a truck overnight and delivered next day, so transport carriers changed the name to 'express' or 'premium'.

Either way, you will receive the fastest possible delivery service which is usually next business day to many areas. This service comes at a premium, and merchants usually limit use to either small products or products with a high-dollar value to allow for the premium shipping cost. Major carriers providing this service include companies like TNT Express, StarTrack Express and Toll.

General and bulk carriers

This segment usually transports full trailer loads or 20 ft × 40 ft containers, as well as pallet loads of all types of products. This isn't an option for a general eCommerce store.

International carriers

We discuss international shipping further in Chapter Three, these types of carriers can import or export products for you internationally. There are postal and express options available, each with benefits and disadvantages. Some of the main players in Australia are TNT Express, DHL Express, DHL eCommerce, Australia Post and FedEx. Sea freight is also a more competitive option for bulk or large products and containers, but this service is not used widely for eCommerce stores.

Local same day and taxi trucks

Both of these segments overlap and are usually provided by the same companies. They mainly deliver within the same local metropolitan area of a city. Examples are postcodes with pick-up and delivery within 2000 to 2232 or 3000 to 3210 or 4000 to 4207. Local same day services are usually for items weighing 1 kg to 250 kg whereas taxi truck services are for items weighing 250 kg to 10,000 kg or more. Both are usually charged either per kilometre or per hour. Carriers like Direct Couriers, Allied Express and Toll Same Day play in this space. The Australian brand Iconic has focused their business model around extensively using same day services for local metro deliveries.

Post

In Australia, it's only Australia Post that provides a postal service domestically at a competitive price.

Furniture removalists

If your product is assembled furniture (eg sofas, dining tables, etc) then furniture removal companies are the only real option as most courier and freight companies will not transport this product. Flat pack furniture is fine to be transported by most courier and freight services.

Drones

We believe the use of drones in the delivery market will be a serious and viable option – in the future. There is much hype globally by Amazon and others trialling delivery of small parcels and pizza delivery, for example, but due to government regulations and safety concerns, there is a lot of planning required to make this happen on a grand scale. Some main issues include high-rise residential apartments, people needing to collect goods from their roofs, potential theft and weather harming packages when left.

Most likely services used by an eCommerce store

Product	Budget shoes	$2,000 handbag	Lounge suite	Pallet of tiles
Road express	✓	✓	X	✓
Express premium	X	✓	X	X
General/bulk carriers	X	X	X	✓
International *	✓	✓	X	X
Local same day	X	✓	X	X
Taxi truck	X	X	✓	✓
Post	✓	X	X	X
Furniture removalists	X	X	✓	X

* International courier services
Information is correct as at year end 2020

Speed of delivery depending on courier

Speed of delivery*	Local metro	Intrastate	Interstate
Road express	Next day	1–5 days	1–10 days
Express premium	Next day	Next day	1–2 days
General/bulk carriers	1–2 days	1–10 days	1–14 days
Local same day	1hr, 2hr, 4hr	N/A	N/A
Taxi truck	1hr, 2hr, 4hr	N/A	N/A
Post	1–2 days	1–5 days	1–10 days
Furniture removalists	Same day	1–5 days	1–14 days

*Business days and a guideline only. Varies by from/to postcodes.
Information is correct as at year end 2020

Going direct vs using a courier aggregator

We recommend for businesses that sell a range of different products (large, medium and small) to review the options available in the marketplace which could improve the level of shipping for your customers and save you substantially on shipping costs.

Think of a courier aggregator as a broker for couriers. Aggregators partner with a number of courier and freight companies. By using an aggregator, you gain access to a wide range of courier services through one online account. Their online quoting options return the best range of shipping quotes from a variety of carriers, saving you time and money without you continually having to research the market. They can also offer you their expertise and advice on which providers may provide the best levels of service depending on your particular product profile and needs.

As mentioned earlier in this chapter, each courier and freight company has strengths and weaknesses in different areas (from price, to network coverage, number of services offered, types of products they can and will transport). By working with a courier aggregator, you get the best of both worlds (ie access to multiple transport companies without having to put all your eggs in the one basket). It also means if a transport company is letting you down with poor service, you can simply choose to use one of the other companies available to you via an aggregator (without any major changes to your system).

Timely 'after despatch customer service' should be offered to you when dealing with an aggregator should issues arise with your shipment. If the aggregator doesn't offer **fast** customer service response times (or no customer service at all), they're just a middleman (ie happy to take your money and offer nothing more) and you should research around for a more professional aggregator that will take away the pain of chasing up delivery issues for you as part of their offering.

Aggregators should also be able to offer technology solutions for your eCommerce business to help you save logistical time and money. We will discuss this in more detail in Chapter Four.

Courier reviews

This can be a touchy subject for many consumers. We have all heard the horror stories about transport companies, courier or delivery drivers, from lost and damaged goods, to items left or thrown over fences, late deliveries, and so on. When researching online and via review sites, the feedback about the industry can look damning; however, when you consider the volume of shipments the Australian transport industry ships every year (we're talking millions upon millions of items), the bad reviews are but a drop in the ocean. The other thing to consider is consumers are quick to leave a bad review because of the pain caused to them but hardly ever leave a good review when all goes to plan.

From our long experience, the transport industry, although not perfect, actually provides a high level of service. Most transport companies go through periods of better and worse levels of service – another reason it helps to work with a courier aggregator.

One of the reasons for poor periods of service is take-overs from larger competitors or overseas companies. We generally find many transport companies struggle in the year or two after a takeover (sometimes for longer periods). The new purchaser reviews the cost base and makes cuts – all too often ripping out middle management – or makes direction changes on the business that is out of whack with the current direction, causing discontent within the workforce.

Takeovers of major Australian transport companies (2010–2020)[11]

Company	Taken over by
StarTrack Express	Australia Post
Toll Ipec	Japan Post
TNT Express	Fedex
Couriers Please	Singapore Post
Fastway Couriers	Aramex

Another reason for periods of lower service levels is changes in customer service departments. Some companies experiment with offshoring their customer service departments to save money. Others had local customer service departments in each state that knew the local layout and customer base well but decided to centralise customer service to one location in Australia. This means slower response times at least initially while the staff work within the new environment – or in the case of offshoring, totally learn the customer service practices from scratch. We have seen many companies get back to normal eventually, but some never recover entirely and continue to provide poor levels of customer service.

Size matters

Small courier companies: You will find they react and respond quicker to your requirements or requests.

---

11   BuiltWith.com

They build personable relationships well and are more hands on. They will, however, lack a large network for delivery capability and must rely on other transport companies to deliver in some areas (particularly regional or rural areas). This means tracking transparency is lacking and pricing can be more expensive in these situations.

Medium courier companies: They sit well in the market with a good range of personable and niche services. Usually, they are privately owned, and the owner is hands on in running the business. They sometimes can get caught in trying to compete with the big companies' infrastructure and services and, due to a lack of cash flow, they can remain stagnant in their offerings for too long.

Large courier companies: They have clear, defined, well-structured services. Service levels are generally good, although they can suffer the troughs discussed earlier with buyouts from even larger companies. Their technology is usually top notch – although not always – and their network of depots around Australia is a great asset with pricing and service deliverability. Flexibility is not always a strength, such as when customers request new features or have custom requests.

There is another aspect to consider: your expectations. As an eCommerce business, you may have certain expectations from your transport provider.

Sometimes these are legitimate and other times they may not be. We'll discuss what's realistic and what's not in the next chapter.

BEWARE OF CROCODILE!

In January 2011, we were commissioned to collect a large crate in Townsville and transit it to Melbourne. As Smart Send is not required to ask the contents of domestic shipments (only whether the goods are dangerous or not), we sent the carrier around to collect the large crate.

In the meantime, torrential rains hit the Queensland coast north of Mackay down the coast, and the Bruce Highway was closed from north of Bundaberg with all freight stopped in their tracks. The large crate was unloaded at the Mackay depot for safe keeping. The carrier's depot was getting ready to flood, so the staff moved all the goods in the depot to dry ground, but this crate was too big, and they popped it in the roof section of the building hoping for the best.

When the flood waters receded, the depot staff climbed into the depot roof to check the crate had stayed dry and safe to get it down. They thought they'd better open the crate to check on the contents. Can you imagine their horror when they discovered a huge seawater crocodile in the crate? Screams were heard until they realised that it was in fact a taxidermy crocodile, and he had some friends travelling with him, a couple of freshwater crocs as well. They nicknamed him Boris and sent him on his way once the highway opened for the trucks.

It took Boris eight weeks to get from Townsville to Melbourne and to his new home, a private collector who loves crocodiles.

The moral of the story: Be careful when unloading large crates!

Summary of key points

In this chapter, we learned:

- How choosing the right transport partner(s) can impact brand image
- The strengths and weaknesses of Australia Post and courier and freight carriers
- The different service types available and why some are better suited to eCommerce than others
- The benefits of courier aggregators
- The reasons for poor courier reviews

THREE
Understanding The Basics

In this chapter, we discuss:

- What's reasonable to expect when shipping
- Delivery options
- The shipping pricing methods
- International shipping
- Deadweight vs cubic weight charging

Reasonable expectations

In our experience people generally have unreasonable expectations of what can and can't be done when shipping or receiving deliveries. This is understandable given the digital age we live in. So, let's get real and outline what is a reasonable expectation and what simply will not happen.

For example, we are asked if the driver will call on approach to a pick-up or delivery, but drivers are not required to call on approach. There are lots of sound reasons for this (although not all of these apply to every carrier):

- The drivers are no longer given company mobile phones.

- They leave the depots early in the mornings with full vans for delivery in addition to pick-up requests they receive throughout the day, so it is difficult to estimate a delivery time as their routes can change throughout the day.

- If they were to stop and call every single delivery, they would not get through their workload for the day.

A call on approach is a specialised service and generally incurs additional costs. Many carriers and Australia Post are beginning to offer SMS or email services though where they will advise receivers that their shipment is 'out for delivery' that day in major metropolitan centres.

People expect to see scanning online every step of the way. However, Australia is a huge, sparsely populated country that cannot be serviced into remote or regional areas by one transport company – not even by Toll, which is one of the biggest logistics companies in the world.

How are these areas serviced? Often, they are serviced via an agent network incorporating smaller, family-owned companies that are engaged to service these areas on the main company's behalf. In some cases, it can be an agent of an agent of an agent. How does this impact you and your customer? Visibility is one potential problem. The agent, as a rule, does not have access to the main companies' scanners to scan the barcodes on the shipping labels. General customer service can be difficult as we all have to wait for the information to come down the line, which in many cases is manually.

Deliveries to offshore islands can be difficult or non-existent. We recommend avoiding sending to offshore islands if possible. Generally speaking, there are no door-to-door deliveries to these addresses. This applies to:

- Moreton Island

- Whitsunday Islands

- Torres Strait Islands

- Bass Strait Islands

To get around this, there is usually a barge or ferry that services the islands, booked to the terminal, and the ferry service will take the goods to their office to be collected by the receiver on the island.

The same would apply to places such as:

- Nhulunbuy

- Weipa

- Remote stations or properties

- Outback communities

Most people living in these offshore islands and remote areas know the system and plan accordingly.

When you have the likes of Australia Post stating they deliver to every address in Australia it can be misleading. Most rural properties would have a PO box at the local post office for mail and smaller items shipped via Australia Post. When delivering to rural areas, most agents will have a drop-off point in town they deliver to. It is price prohibitive to have a driver drive out to a rural property outside of a small town to deliver one shipment: let's say it's thirty minutes each way, that's an hour of the driver's time, minimum cost estimate $60. In some cases, the agent's share of the delivery fee could be as small as $2. Once you're aware, it's easy to understand why these addresses have no door-to-door service.

Gated communities and apartment buildings are secure living arrangements in today's modern world. We all want to feel safe and secure in our homes. They do, however, present issues for the delivery drivers who cannot gain access to the property and the receiver's door. The driver is only allocated a short time for each delivery; this is so they can effect as many deliveries as possible in any given day. So, let's break down the issues for gated communities:

- The driver cannot gain access without a security code.

- The driver needs to stop and get out of their vehicle to key in the unit number.

- Hopefully someone answers and opens the gate, and the driver returns to his vehicle and drives in.

All this takes enormous amounts of time when added up throughout the day and what happens if no one is home? No one wants their goods left on the letterboxes or at the gate. Someone is likely to come along and take them. It's not secure and is a major issue for the carriers and eCommerce industry.

An apartment building offers many of the same problems and is sometimes harder:

- The driver has to be able to park which is often not possible for city apartment buildings.

- The driver has to buzz the apartment and hope someone is able to let them in.

- They cannot gain access to the lifts to the apartment (and who wants their goods left at their door in the hallway?).

- Often with apartments, the driver cannot access the mailboxes to leave a card to advise the receiver they have attempted the delivery and what to do next to get their goods.

It's frustrating for drivers, annoying for the end receiver waiting for the goods and time consuming and costly for you if the goods get returned.

Many transport companies have solutions for this in place:

- Couriers Please has POPshops or POPstations.

- Fastway / Aramex has Parcel Connect.

- TNT/Fedex has Local Connect.

- Toll Group has Toll Collection Points (TCP), also described as Alternate Delivery Points (ADP).

- Australia Post has parcel lockers.

All of these are great solutions and give you and your customer secure options should delivery not be possible.

One important point to reinforce with your customers is couriers and freight companies cannot deliver to PO boxes or parcel lockers as this is the domain of Australia Post. If you're using courier/freight services for your business, be sure to ask the customer for a street address for delivery (this can be as easy as a header notification on your webstore or checkout, or a message in your eBay listing), otherwise there will be delays and possibly further costs incurred to correct a delivery marked to a PO box or parcel locker.

In some cases, the carrier will automatically deliver to the local collection point if the driver cannot deliver the goods safely. In some locations though there won't be a local drop or collection point where the driver can deliver the goods to. If the receiver lives in a gated community or secure apartment building, it would be best to mention to the receiver to keep an eye on the tracking of their order, just in case the driver cannot access the mailboxes for the building due to security gates. If there is not an available drop point, the goods will be returned to the carrier's depot, at which point redelivery arrangements need to be made.

Delivery options

When you place a booking, you need to consider what delivery options are available.

The most common delivery option these days is giving the driver an authority to leave (ATL). What does this mean? You have given the driver the authority to leave the goods if no one is available to sign for the shipment.

The ATL option has:

Pros

- If the receiver is out and about a lot (and is unlikely to be available to sign for and accept the goods), the driver can leave safely at the front door.

- If it's a small parcel, the driver will generally leave in the letter box.

- You, as the merchant, won't incur any further redelivery charges as the shipment is considered delivered.

Cons

- If goods are left at the front door, this is great if the receiver is in a nice neighbourhood with a low crime rate. The downside is if the front of the house is open to the street or has easy access and anyone can see the goods sitting there ... well, you know the rest.

- You cannot make a claim for loss of goods if an ATL service is used. You take the risk that leaving the goods at the delivery address means the shipment has been delivered. If it goes missing after the fact, then there is no recourse.

Your other option is to request a signature on delivery (or receipted delivery) service. A signature on delivery option comes with pros and cons as well.

Pros

- The driver cannot leave the goods unattended at the door without obtaining a signature. If they do, generally speaking, the driver will be held accountable for the value of the goods as they cannot verify delivery.

- Anyone at the delivery address can sign for the goods (not just the person named as the delivery contact on the shipment paperwork). This then means delivery has occurred.

- Greater transparency for all parties as the signature proves there is no doubt the goods have been delivered.

Cons

- There can be delays in the customer getting their goods. For example, if the driver has attempted delivery and no one is available to sign for the goods, the driver will leave a 'sorry we missed you card' in the letter box advising the receiver how to arrange redelivery of the goods on a suitable day (or collect from a collection point). Once this contact has been made, most carriers will need two business days to get the goods out for delivery again.

- Choosing a signature upon delivery option over an ATL will usually also incur additional charges.

Why would you select one over the other? The value of the item has a role to play. If your goods are inexpensive and easy to replace if the receiver claims non-delivery, then the ATL option works well. The incident of loss is small. It's not a huge impact on your business if you find yourself having to reship every now and then. Plus, you won't need to pay the additional charges for a signature on delivery service for shipments.

It is different if the goods are valuable, difficult to source or costly to reship. The impact on your business could be substantial. If you definitely want to know the receiver has received the goods, we advise a signature on delivery option should be used.

There are situations that could change this, such as the SMS or email from the carrier or Australia Post, telling the receiver their parcel is coming today with three options for delivery:

- No one is home to sign for the goods, please deliver on _____.

- No one is available to sign for the goods, please leave at the door.

- Please deliver to the closest post office or collection point.

If the receiver chooses the ATL option (the second option) over your originally selected signature on delivery, then the carrier has the authority for the driver to leave the goods and you have no recourse against the carrier (if the receiver ever claimed non-delivery). We have seen this situation get nasty, and it can end up costing you dearly, which is not ideal.

We would suggest, if possible, to arrange delivery to a business address for your customer. This will eliminate lots of the headaches outlined above.

Shipping pricing methods

There are a few different methods couriers and freight companies and Australia Post use to calculate shipping charges. You need to be aware of these methods as you could be overpaying for your shipping based on your current provider's method.

The main formats are:

- Basic charge plus per kilogram rate
- Per item or per satchel
- Pallet rate
- Weight break

Basic charge and per kilogram rate

This method is used widely in the courier and freight industry, and is one of the most common formats. When sending a consignment, they charge a basic charge for the entire consignment sent (irrespective of whether you are sending one item or twenty items), and you also pay a charge per kilogram sent. The per kilogram amount is calculated from the greater of the deadweight or cubic weight of the items sent in the consignment (see 'Deadweight vs cubic weight' below in this chapter).

Example: You send two stereo speakers in two boxes at 10 kg deadweight, 60 cm × 30 cm × 20 cm each.

Basic charge: $10 + $0.40 per kg

Total charge weight = 20 kg

Basic charge: $10 + (20 kg × $0.40) = $18.00 (exclusive of fuel levy and goods and service tax (GST))

Per item rate

This method is usually most competitive for single item consignments as there is just one charge per item sent. Often there are different per item rates provided based on the charge weight sent (eg 0 kg to 1 kg, 1.01 kg to 3 kg, 3.01 kg to 5 kg, 5.01 kg to 10 kg, etc).

Example: You send one skateboard in a carton/box at 6 kg, 60 cm × 30 cm × 20 cm.

Per item rate: 5.01 kg to 10 kg category = $15

One item × $15 = $15.00 (exclusive of
fuel levy and GST)

Pallet rate

Some freight companies will provide a price per pallet sent. This is similar to a per item rate method, but only for heavy products sent on pallets. Usually, the company will require the merchant to ensure the product on the pallet does not 'overhang' the pallet and must fit squarely on a standard pallet (a standard pallet is 117 cm × 117 cm at the base). The reason freight companies offer better pricing as a pallet rate is because they can load the pallet alongside other pallets in their linehaul vehicles (two standard pallets fit the width of a linehaul vehicle) avoiding inefficiencies (and lost space in their vehicles) when loading and shipping these heavy and bulky items.

Weight break

Commonly used for bulk or heavy consignments (eg pallets of stock, crates, etc) by bulk or general carriers. There are sliding scales of pricing based on the charge weight sent in the consignment (eg 0–250 kg, 251–500 kg, 501–1000 kg, 1001–3000 kg, etc) as well as a basic charge per consignment sent. It's not a common option utilised for eCommerce stores unless you're selling heavy or large products (eg pallets of tiles, crated machinery, etc).

Example: You send a pallet of tiles at 600 kg, 120 cm × 120 × 160 cm.

Weight break rate: basic charge $20 + per kg rate (0–250 kg = $0.22, 251–500 kg = $0.17, 501 kg to 1,000 kg = $0.14, 1,001 kg to 3,000 kg = $0.12)

Basic charge: $20 + (600 kg × $0.14) = $104 exclusive Fuel Levy & GST

It may seem difficult to work out the best option for your product as different carriers use different methods. The beauty of working with a courier aggregator is smart algorithms are used in their online quoting systems to work all this out for you in real time. Quotes are returned for each courier and freight company along with delivery timeframes and all you need to do is choose the best option for your requirements.

International shipping

According to a 2019 Australia Post eCommerce report, the global online goods market is forecast to reach $US3.4 trillion by 2023 (up around 100% from 2018 figures).[12] It's a huge opportunity for Australian merchants, opening your business up to a massive global population.

The biggest buyers for Australian products seem to be New Zealanders (29%), China (15%) and India (11%).[13] Per transaction 22% spent between $35 to $69, 21% spent over $150 and 10% spent over $300.[14]

Shipping internationally requires some research and can be a bit of a minefield depending on the products you sell. Every country has different regulations on incoming products. If you work with a good partner or carrier, they will be able to assist you.

The part that is easier to calculate is shipping pricing as most international courier and post providers charge by country and charge weight. As long as you can work out the charge weight, you can look up the destination country and figure out the price.

12　Australia Post, *Inside Australian online shopping: 2019 eCommerce Industry Report* (Australia Post, 2019), https://auspost.com.au/content/dam/auspost_corp/media/documents/inside-australian-online-shopping-ecommerce-report.pdf, accessed 25 January 2021

13　Ibid

14　Ibid

Postal and courier services for international delivery

There are a few things to be aware of with international services. For international postal, these are low-cost services great for low-value items or small items (generally under 2 kg charge weight). When the goods arrive at the destination country they go into the local postal network and, in most cases, there is no or limited tracking and transparency of where your goods are (apart from a few major countries). If an item goes missing, many times it stays missing. With postal services, the delivery timeframe to many countries (apart from New Zealand) can be up to two weeks or, in some cases, longer.

For international courier services, the cost is much more but the delivery timeframe is also much faster. We find most countries are delivered within four business days or quicker (excluding some small or unpopular countries). The goods stay within the network of these international express couriers which means you will know where the goods are at all times and can track them for peace of mind. If you are a strong brand or have mid- to high-value products, we strongly recommend only using courier and express options for international or at least offer a tracked and untracked shipping option at checkout on your site, allowing the buyer to choose their preference.

The other option is sea freight. This is primarily for bulk, heavy items, pallets or 20-foot by 40-foot containers of goods. Sea freight doesn't cater to normal eCommerce deliveries of parcels, satchels, cartons, etc as minimum charges are high and delivery is slow.

The main Australian international courier/post options for eCommerce

	Postal	Courier
Australia Post	✓	✓
DHL Express	X	✓
DHL eCommerce	✓	✓
TNT Express	X	✓
FedEx	X	✓
UPS	X	✓
Toll Global Express	X	✓

Information is correct as at year end 2020

Common international shipping issues

Restricted items: The list is extensive and can be dependent on the destination country, but the main items that most international courier and post providers will not transport are dangerous or hazardous goods (eg flammable, batteries, explosives, weapons, aerosols, etc). These items may be able to be transported via sea freight however (contact a freight forwarder for assistance).

Duties: One big thing to consider is customs duties are payable at the destination country (some postal services for low value items don't require duties to be paid). We strongly recommend advising your international customers that they will need to pay the duties when the goods arrive at their country. They will be notified by the local authorities on the amount to be paid and then delivery can occur. Most international courier and post providers prefer this process. It is difficult for you to pay the duties as the sender as you'll need to work out how much the duties will be. This can be time consuming and cause delays for your business and orders.

Either way, the onus is on you as the consignor to pay the duties if the receiver refuses to pay, and you will also incur 'return to sender' charges (which can be expensive) if either party doesn't pay the duties. Therefore, it is in your best interests to be upfront with the buyer when they are purchasing from you and put it in writing that they must pay the duties at their end.

Paperwork: When shipping internationally there is more paperwork required than when shipping domestically. You need to provide information such as:

- Consignment label
- Consignment note/airwaybill including tax status, export reason and tax file number

- Customs invoice including information such as quantity of items, description of contents, country of manufacture, unit value, harmonised code (optional for most countries), total weight, total number of packages, unit value and total value

You should provide a clear and accurate description of the goods you are shipping. Vague or inaccurate descriptions may result in the shipment being held by customs, resulting in delayed deliveries and additional surcharges for item inspection and/or incomplete data.

When shipping to New Zealand, for items with a declared value greater than NZ$400 and less than NZ$1,000, a New Zealand Full Tariff code is required. Go to www.tariff-finder.govt.nz to generate your tariff code.

It sounds daunting; however, if you work with a good partner or carrier, it's just a matter of filling out their online form questions when sending the goods and their system will generate all the required paperwork for you to print and have ready to ship the goods.

Deadweight vs cubic weight

When carriers calculate the 'charge weight' of your shipped products, they will charge the greater of the deadweight or cubic weight of the item. Deadweight is the actual weight of the item when placed on weighing scales (note Australian carriers use kilograms for weight calculation). Cubic weight is a weight derived from the cubic volume of the shipped item.

Most road express, express premium and local metro carriers and Australia Post use a cubic conversion rate of 250 kg/m³. Most bulk/general carriers use 333 kg/m³. International carriers can vary but most from our experience use 200 kg/m³. In most cases, as an eCommerce store you will be using 250 kg/m³ as the conversion rate. Australian carriers use centimetres for dimensions and when working out the cubic weight, you should convert the dimensions to metreage (see example below). Here is an example of a calculation where cubic weight is greater than the deadweight.

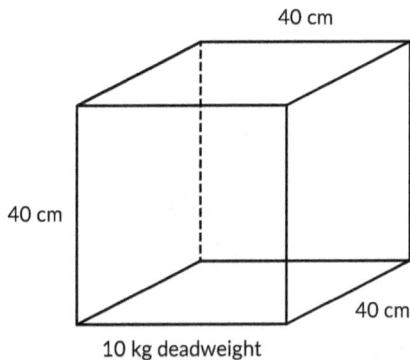

40 cm

40 cm

40 cm

10 kg deadweight

Cubic weight vs deadweight

- Length = 40 cm

- Width = 40 cm

- Height = 40 cm

- Deadweight = 10 kg

- Formula: $0.40 \times 0.40 \times 0.40 \times 250$ kg / m^3 = 16 kg

As the cubic weight of 16 kg is greater than the deadweight of 10 kg, the carrier will charge you at 16 kg in this example.

What if you have weird-shaped products? For a pyramid shape you would calculate the base as length by width. The height is the height. You may ask, 'What about all the air I'm not using around the height?' The carrier will still charge you for that space because they can't realistically package other customers' products in that space efficiently or at all when they load everyone's products into their linehaul vehicles for carriage. Every bit of empty space is lost revenue for carriers, so they need to ensure they can load all products into their vehicles efficiently and as tightly as possible.

Here is an online cubic conversion calculator you can use on the Toll Group website: www.tollgroup.com/tools/cubic-volumetric-calculator.

> ## TOP TIP: SAVE MORE WHEN SHIPPING
>
> Want to save even more when shipping? The secret is to make your package, satchel, carton, pallet, etc as dense as possible. The more air you have inside your package when sent, the likelier you are to pay more for your shipment. Be careful you don't sacrifice internal packaging to save on shipping costs though. Packaging your goods appropriately is important, otherwise skimping on internal packaging could hurt you more in the long run with increased damage rates (for more on this, see Chapter Four).

TAKING MEASUREMENTS

Julie would regularly ship small boxes of product in courier satchels. The box was around 20 cm × 15 cm × 10 cm in size and she would place this box inside a courier satchel that was 40 cm × 20 cm × 10 cm when sent. She would declare the size at 20 cm × 15 cm × 10 cm when shipping.

Julie didn't realise the courier company used automated machinery to check the cubic volume of the items sent and began receiving ongoing extra charges for her shipments because the charge weight was greater than she had booked and planned for. The measurements were coming through at the satchel size which was larger than she had declared.

The moral of the story: Always accurately declare your package's measurements to avoid incurring surcharges and extra fees.

Automated checking machinery

All carriers now use specialised machinery to automatically check the deadweight and cubic volume of items sent. Gone are the days of pick-up drivers or operations staff manually using a tape measure. The machinery is embedded into a conveyor belt that sorts packages in transport depots (see image below). As the item goes through the machine, it is weighed, and lasers measure the three dimensions of the item. This all happens quickly in real time with thousands of items being checked per hour. Any discrepancies are then notified to you on your next invoice with further charges to be paid.

The technology is extremely accurate; however, false scans of the dimensions can occur occasionally with the lasers if packaging tape is loose on the package or the edge of a carton has come loose or the package is squashed out of shape, etc. It pays to ensure the packages leave your premises neatly taped up and in a robust package, carton, etc to ensure none of these potential issues can occur. You usually can dispute the carrier's findings if you provide evidence of the item sent.

Dimensioner machine embedded in a conveyor belt

How to beat the machine

Experienced shippers from time to time may have received additional charges after delivery because the goods travelled through the carrier's Dimensioner machine and were found to be under-declared at the time of booking. We cannot stress enough how important it is to declare the dead weight and dimensions correctly when shipping goods.

Each carrier has a freight profile, if you under-declare the weight or dimensions to try to save a few dollars on shipping, all you will get is delays, additional costs or futile pick-up fees.

The transport company needs to know the correct dead weight and dimensions so they can send the right sized vehicle and staff aren't injured loading a heavy item that was declared as a lighter item. Huge fines can apply to senders, carriers and anyone in the logistics supply chain as part of the Chain of Responsibility legislation (if incorrect declarations are made when shipping). You can read up more about this important topic at https://www.nhvr.gov.au/safety-accreditation-compliance/chain-of-responsibility.

To stop false scans by the lasers used by the Dimensioner machine, it is important to ensure:

- Your barcoded shipping labels are flat on the carton and not crinkled

- There is no packaging tape sitting up from the package and the tape is nice and flat

- If you add strapping around cartons/boxes/ flat packs, the strapping is nice and tight (ie not sitting up from the package or loose)

It will be up to you to prove the Dimensioner is wrong. It's time consuming and can be costly. In some cases, the carrier may hold your goods in transit until the matter is resolved – this is rare but can happen.

To protect yourself, use standard sized cartons for shipping (small, medium or large depending on your product range). If you are then brought into question, you can quickly and easily provide evidence that on this occasion, the carrier has got it wrong.

By law, the carriers are required to have their Dimensioner machines calibrated regularly to ensure the information is collected correctly.

Summary of key points

In this chapter, we learned:

- Reasonable expectations to have when shipping

- Whether ATL or signature on delivery is best depending on product profile

- An understanding of the various methods to calculate shipping costs

- What to consider when shipping internationally

- Tips on how to potentially save on shipping costs over the long term including whether to charge on deadweight or cubic weight

- Tips to minimise incorrect scans and charges from Dimensioner machines

FOUR

Be Aware: Extras And Add-ons

In this chapter, we discuss:

- Surcharges in transport
- Insurance and whether it is worth it
- Dangerous and hazardous goods

Surcharges in transport

We're all weary of reading the fine print when signing an agreement. There always seem to be extra charges that come out of nowhere. In transport, they're most likely spelled out for you in the agreement, but you probably don't know what they mean until you incur them.

The main additional charges to watch out for are:

- Goods and service tax

- Fuel levy

- Security surcharge

- Redelivery charge

- Redirection charge

- Return to Sender charge

- Oversize/length surcharge

- Overweight surcharge

- Residential delivery surcharge

- Residential pick-up surcharge

- Remote surcharge

- Dangerous/hazardous goods surcharge

- Manual consignment note charge/non-electronic consignment fee

- Manual handling surcharge

- Under-declared item charge/manual measurement fee

- Waiting time charge

- Futile pick-up charge

- Account servicing fee

- Early delivery charge

- Pre-alert charge

- Book-in/time slot delivery charge

GST

Nearly all transport carriers quote their services/rate cards excluding GST. It will state this in the fine print, but it is best to confirm this with their sales representative. The exception may be if you are receiving quotes via an online portal where these should include GST but be careful as sometimes GST is excluded and is only added on when you're booking your job online or making payment.

Fuel levy

This charge started around twenty-five years ago. Transport companies generally increase their courier and freight charges annually for customers. They began to realise increasing their courier and freight prices annually didn't help their bottom line during the year if oil and fuel prices began to rise. Fuel expenditure for a transport company is a huge cost, so a fuel levy percentage charge was introduced that could fluctuate throughout the year (usually updated monthly) should oil and fuel prices impact their margins. When negotiating, ask the sales rep what the current fuel levy is, how often do they amend the percentage and how are you notified.

Security surcharge

This is similar to a fuel levy and was introduced by some carriers about twenty years ago. It usually only applies for express or air services for carriers in Australia and helps recover costs associated with providing security aspects of air carriage.

Redelivery charge

This charge is to redeliver goods should the delivery driver not be able to deliver your consignment to the receiver. You can minimise this fee by choosing an ATL (or no signature required) service when booking with your provider, and the driver can leave the goods at a safe location at the delivery address. The amount varies by provider so best to check when first signing up and factor a small percentage into the shipping pricing you pass on to your customers. You should evaluate over time how often you receive redelivery charges and then update the small percentage in your shipping charges.

Redirection charge

This charge applies if you accidentally entered the wrong delivery address or need to change the delivery address after despatching the goods. Once the goods are in the carrier's system, there are costs and time involved in redirecting the consignment to the correct delivery address. The carrier has not factored this into their original pricing, so these costs are borne after the fact when you notify them of the correction required.

The charge can vary greatly depending on what type of redirection is required. For example, if you booked goods to go from Brisbane to Perth and four days after despatch you realise you should have sent the order to Cairns, it is likely that the carrier will charge from Perth back to Cairns, which will be an expensive exercise. In addition, you will lose the original amount paid. This is because the goods are probably in a container on the Nullarbor Plain and can't be touched until they arrive at the carrier's Perth depot.

TOP TIP: HOW TO AVOID DELIVERY ADDRESS ERRORS

One way to minimise incorrect delivery addresses is to use 'address verification' services on your website when customers check out (this way your customer can't misspell their address as they need to choose the correct address from a list of options once they start typing). Google has a free street address option your developer can add to your checkout.

Return to sender charge

This charge happens when the receiver of your order has refused delivery. This could be because the package was damaged, the receiver wasn't happy with the order or they were unhappy with how long it took to receive the order. Alternatively, you may have asked for the package to be returned to you as it was incorrect. (Incidentally, the delivery driver doesn't have to wait and allow the receiver to open the package(s) upon delivery to inspect the goods; the driver is on a strict time limit and has many stops on their run each day.) Sometimes the 'return to sender' charge may apply because the delivery couldn't be made (no one home) and there was no response from the receiver when contacted to collect their goods. In some cases, you may be able to dispute this charge with your provider if the fault lies with their service.

Oversize/length surcharge

Transport carriers and Australia Post have different preferences for the types of goods they want to transport. This comes down to their systems, depots and types of vehicles they use. When an item gets to be over a certain length, it can cost some providers more than they planned for in their pricing. This is because their system may cater to smaller parcels only and the conveyor belts (and corners in the conveyor belts) only cater for an item that is so big. Similarly, they may only use smaller vehicles or vans to deliver the shipments whereas other companies use larger trucks.

Common cut-offs we have seen start from 1 m (eg Australia Post) to 1.2 m, 1.5 m, 2 m and 3 m depending on the courier or freight carrier. If your item has a length longer than the cut-off, you will incur a surcharge on top of the normal pricing. This surcharge can vary anywhere from $5 up to $100 for very long items. When negotiating, be sure to check what the carrier's surcharges are and factor them into your shipping pricing.

Overweight surcharge

The maximum weight allowed per item by carriers has been decreasing over the past five years. Where before carriers were happy to transport any item without specialised assistance, now you will need to provide loading/unloading machinery or pay extra for the privilege to ship your heavy item. The cut-offs we're seeing are 22 kg for Australia Post and 25 kg to 30 kg for couriers and freight carriers. Once an item gets over 25 kg to 30 kg you need to provide a forklift to load or unload the item. This is because of ever-increasing occupational health and safety (OHS) issues with drivers being injured lifting heavy items and legal issues with consumers being injured trying to assist with unloading heavy items from vehicles.

If you don't have a forklift available at pick-up and delivery address (unlikely for many small and medium eCommerce businesses), you need to request a tail-lift truck or two-man service when booking the shipment. A tail-lift truck is a vehicle that has a tail-lifter on the back door which lowers to the ground and allows the driver to easily lower or lift heavy items up to truck level to get it on safely without anyone having to lift the heavy item. These services come at an additional cost to you. We highly recommend using these services for the benefit of all and particularly to ensure you get a positive customer review when your shipment is delivered safely.

What you don't want is the heavy item being dropped or pushed off the back of the truck and being damaged, or the carrier refusing to work with you again should you choose not to use these services for your heavy products (in many cases they will charge you for the extra service anyway even if you didn't book it).

When you use online systems or courier aggregators to book your shipments, you can request these services and the price quote returned includes all these charges in advance so you can quote your customer correctly.

Residential delivery/pick-up surcharge

Up until ten to fifteen years ago, courier and freight carriers in Australia only did business to business (B2B) deliveries. In fact, they hated doing residential deliveries or pick-ups, and mostly refused to do them.

Smart Send, being the first online courier aggregator in Australia, actually pulled the major transport companies kicking and screaming into the home delivery age. It took a number of years to reinforce the future of home deliveries and eCommerce and eventually the couriers we use came onboard and began offering these services.

Many of the companies began to realise the cost involved with picking up and delivering at a residential address was higher than a commercial address. This is because drivers picking up from or delivering to commercial precincts or suburbs had multiple customers and shipments to service which meant cost effectiveness for the carrier. When doing a residential job, they often had minimal other jobs nearby, hence the travel time to go to and from the residential suburb increased as did their costs. Many carriers charge a fee to pick up or deliver to a residential suburb. Running your business from home is still considered a residential job and you will be charged a residential charge per consignment sent, but not all couriers charge this fee. The charges vary by carrier anywhere from $5 up to $100 or more for very heavy shipments, so check with your provider before signing up to factor these costs in.

Remote surcharge

This surcharge applies for remote and rural areas where the costs to deliver or pick up are high because of the address's remoteness. Sometimes carriers don't service the area themselves and need to engage other agents or partners to collect and deliver for them which comes at an additional cost. Some carriers incorporate this charge into their zone pricing on their rate cards, while other times they simply apply a remote surcharge to the shipment sent.

Dangerous/hazardous goods surcharge

Be aware that when sending any form of dangerous/hazardous goods you will incur a surcharge by the carriers that move these products (we cover which goods are dangerous/hazardous later in this chapter). Some carriers refuse to transport dangerous goods products as there is much training and ongoing certification necessary to be able to move these goods. In addition, there are huge fines for carriers and consignors who incorrectly ship dangerous goods products. As a result, many carriers choose not to get involved. The government provides links to local state authorities and guidelines on transporting dangerous/hazardous goods: www.infrastructure. gov.au/transport/australia/dangerous/transport_ dangerous_goods.aspx.

Manual consignment note charge/non-electronic consignment fee

When Steven started in transport over twenty-seven years ago, consignors had to manually complete consignment notes and had three or four copies for each party (sender copy, invoice copy, carrier operation's copy and proof of delivery copy). Today, nearly every carrier requires customers to use online booking portals or software to generate shipping labels, manifests and transfer booking data via electronic transfer. If there ever is a need to manually complete a consignment note, the carrier will now charge you for the privilege as the processing of these costs them more time and money. Charges can be from $5 up to $20 in some cases. Non-electronic consignment fees are similar to manual consignment note fees and apply if you do not electronically send consignment data to the carrier or do not send the data on time.

Manual handling surcharge

This is a fairly new surcharge introduced by some carriers. The terminology around it can vary, but generally it applies if you send awkwardly packaged goods, a product that is not packaged well or items that can't easily travel down the conveyor belts in their depots to be sorted automatically (the industry calls this 'ugly freight'). If manual intervention is required to sort the product through the depot, manually measure the weight and dimensions or any other form of inconvenience to the carrier, then you will experience this surcharge. The best way to not incur this charge is to package your goods in neat square, rectangular or circular packaging that is self-sustained (ie if other product is placed on top of it in transit, it will sustain the load or not cause movement). Using normal cartons, boxes and parcels is usually fine as long as they aren't overly long in size. Just wrapping product in cardboard will most likely be an issue.

Under-declared item charge/manual measurement fee

This one isn't actually a surcharge but is important to be aware of. This charge applies if you under-declare the deadweight or cubic weight of the goods sent. As discussed in Chapter Three the carriers check all goods sent to ensure they are receiving the correct revenue. If you under-declare the deadweight or dimensions, they will charge you for the correct amount of the shipment based on the correct deadweight or dimensions. Some carriers also charge a manual measurement fee to the customer. We strongly recommend declaring the weight and dimensions of your products correctly as if you're found to continually do the wrong thing, the carrier or provider may refuse to transport goods for you in the future.

Waiting time charge

If a driver has to wait beyond an acceptable amount of time to pick up or deliver goods (due to no fault of the driver), then you may incur a waiting time charge. The amount of time varies by carrier, but five minutes is a good average. If this charge applies, it's usually at the pick-up address and it's rare to occur at the delivery address (although can happen).

Futile pick-up charge

If a driver arrives to collect goods for a shipment and cannot collect the goods (eg sender not home, goods are not ready to be shipped, unpackaged or not appropriately packaged, etc), then you will incur a futile pick-up charge. This can vary from $5 to $25.

Account servicing fee

This is applied per invoice sent. Some carriers charge weekly, others fortnightly or monthly. The charge can vary from $2 to $20 per invoice.

Early delivery charge

Most carriers deliver goods between 9am to 5pm weekdays. If you require goods to be delivered earlier than 9am, this can be arranged but there is a surcharge as a specialised driver is required to deliver the consignment outside a normal run. Charges vary widely but can start from $20 up to $100 per consignment.

Pre-alert charge

Some carriers offer the option to pre-alert a receiver that goods are out for delivery that day if you prefer. This can occur via an SMS message, email or a phone call. Depending on the choices offered by your provider, the cost will vary from no charge up to $5 or more per consignment.

Book in/time slot delivery charge

If you seal a deal with large chain stores or department stores, you will need to deliver to their distribution centres or warehouses and these larger deliveries (pallets or containers) will need to be booked in for a particular time slot delivery by the carrier. To arrange the time slot delivery or organise a specific vehicle to deliver during that time, the carrier will charge you a book in or time slot delivery charge. Prices generally vary from $20 up to $100 per consignment.

This may sound like a minefield to navigate, but careful planning and dealing with reputable and professional carriers and courier aggregators can minimise the potential costs and extra charges and give you peace of mind. Like most things in life, it's about building strong relationships – processes and procedures are much easier to navigate if you have solid contacts to draw on during your partnership.

Insurance in transport

Most carriers and Australia Post will provide an option to cover your goods against loss and damage, though it may not be called insurance.

Consider insuring your goods if:

- You are sending high-value, fragile and/or heavy or awkward products (checking first that your product is covered by the carrier's terms)

- You're a well-known brand

- It is part of your 'shipping strategy'

From our experience, there are certain things to consider which cause insurance claims to be made when shipping, including:

- Poor packaging – internal or external (leading to damage – more on this in Chapter Five)

- Shipping labels coming off the package (if you can, use two shipping labels on the package)

- ATL situations where goods are later stolen (consider using signature on delivery services)

You may find an excess still applies to claim pay-outs, so query this with your provider when signing up. Some providers also provide a level of free cover up to a certain monetary threshold.

When making a claim, you will need to provide a wholesale invoice for the cost of the goods. This is not the retail value of the goods when you sold them to your customer, but the amount you paid for the goods (or what it cost to manufacture). The claims process can also take some time to complete from a couple of weeks up to three months. In this case, to avoid receiving bad reviews, send out replacement goods to your buyer.

The cost to cover goods can be on the expensive side with some carriers. If you're sending a decent volume of goods annually, you may want to investigate obtaining your own marine transit policy to cover your goods through an insurance broker. This may be a better option to cover all your goods in transit at a better price than paying individually per consignment, and it will give you peace of mind should something go wrong.

Dangerous goods

Not all dangerous goods are obvious, so you need to be aware of what you need to declare. The fines and penalties for not declaring any dangerous goods can be huge, up to $500,000 for an individual. The following list* cannot be transported in Australia without being declared as dangerous/hazardous goods:

- Batteries
    - Lithium – laptop computers, mobile phones, remote-controlled toys, drones, electric bikes or scooters, etc (in some cases lithium batteries can be shipped normally but check first with your provider)

- Car (dry cell or not)

• Perfumes or aftershaves

• Hand sanitisers (small quantities)

• Essential oils

• Aerosols

• Guns

• Other weapons – arrows, swords, etc

• Gas bottles – including small gas cylinders, scuba tanks, oxygen tanks (even empty)

• Paint

• Flammable items

• Anything toxic

• Explosives

• Anything corrosive

• Some cleaning chemicals

• Pool chemicals

*This list is not comprehensive. Please check with the local dangerous goods authority in your state for more information.

HIDDEN HAZARDS

Years ago, we worked with a start-up online business selling equipment for swimming pools including toys, skimmers, cleaners and, unknown to us at the time, pool chemicals. While most of the items were fine to ship without having to declare as dangerous goods, when the company tried to air freight some pool testing chemicals, they were identified by the carrier and the Civil Aviation Safety Authority (CASA) became involved. It was a messy affair for all involved.

The moral of the story: Make sure you claim all dangerous goods.

Not knowing what is a dangerous good and what isn't is no excuse, and the ramifications to yourself and your business are simply not worth the risks.

Summary of key points

In this chapter, we learned:

- About common surcharges in transport

- How transport insurance works

- The importance of understanding if products are classified as dangerous/hazardous goods

FIVE
Packing For Success

In this chapter, we discuss:

• Which products are easier to ship than others

• Packaging solutions for successful shipping

• Lean and green packaging options

Pick easy to ship products

When sourcing your product line, always keep in the back of your mind what, if any, extra packaging you'll need for the goods to arrive intact to the receiver.

Let's pick an industry such as homewares, which is big business these days. We'll take a look at what we'd consider easy to ship and what isn't.

Easy to ship

Soft furnishings like throw rugs, cushions, bedspreads, pillows. You can easily ship any of these in a satchel and know they will arrive to your customer safely.

Not so easy

You need to consider your packaging and shipping options for products like vases, paintings, ceramics, picture frames, glassware, etc. All of these items are highly fragile and will require extra packaging internally to ensure they are given some shockability (packaging that will absorb the shock if the carton sustains a knock while in transit) and a robust double or triple walled carton or box as the outer packaging.

Let's look at some products (sold as new) that can and can't be shipped easily in eCommerce situations.

Easy and not so easy to ship products

Product	Easy to ship?	Comments
Aerosols	X	Dangerous goods, must be declared
Artwork/ sculptures	X	Artwork is hard to insure, if at all

Product	Easy to ship?	Comments
Automotive parts	✓	Must be clean of all grease, oil and fuels
Baby products	✓	Cots must be flat packed
Batteries	X	Requires dangerous goods paperwork, signage/labels, additional charges apply
BBQ	✓	Must be packed into carton, each under 30 kg, or a tail-lift is required
Beds	✓	Only flat-packed frames
Bicycle	✓	Must be in a bike carton
Blinds	✓	Must be in cartons
Books	✓	Must be in carton or satchel
Bumper bars	✓	Must be in purpose-built cartons
Car panels	✓	Must be in purpose-built cartons with internal protection
Chairs	✓	Dining and outdoor chairs must be in cartons
Computers/ laptops	✓	Lithium batteries found in most computers are classified as dangerous/ hazardous goods, dangerous goods paperwork, signage/ labels and additional charges may apply
Cookware	✓	Must be in cartons

Product	Easy to ship?	Comments
Dangerous/ hazardous goods	X	Requires dangerous goods paperwork, signage/labels and additional charges apply
Fashion clothing	✓	Must be in satchel or parcel
Foodstuffs	✓	Perishable foodstuffs generally can't be sent with many courier and freight companies
Furniture	✓	Must be well packaged in flat pack or cartons only and non-packaged furniture (eg sofas, dining tables, etc) should be sent with furniture removalists
Gas bottles (full or empty)	X	Are classified as dangerous/hazardous goods, dangerous goods paperwork, signage/ labels and additional charges apply
Glass products	X	Need to be in exceptional internal and external packaging to avoid damage
Hi-Fi equipment	✓	Needs to be in cartons
Homewares	✓	Soft furnishings are fine and fragile homewares should be packaged with good internal and external packaging

Product	Easy to ship?	Comments
Liquids	X	Sending liquid product can limit the number of carriers you have access to, but if you are a regular or larger sender of these items, some carriers will transport them
Luggage	✓	Must be in cartons
Mattresses	X	Must be in cartons and requires two-person handling
Musical instruments	✓	As long as they are in their hardcase and sent inside an external carton or box
Porcelain sinks	X	As fragile and heavy, good internal packaging is the key to safe delivery
Sporting equipment	✓	Must be in cartons
Televisions	✓	Must be in cartons with original internal packaging
Tiles	X	Fragile and need internal support to avoid breakages
Toilets	X	Heavy and fragile and need internal support and protection
Towbars	✓	Must be in cartons only
Vanity units	X	Must be in cartons (same as toilets)

Product	Easy to ship?	Comments
Whitegoods	✓	If over 25 kg to 30 kg a tail-lift truck delivery service will need to be used
Wine	✓	Package using cardboard dividers in wine cartons

Wine and alcohol: Many feel comfortable buying our wine online these days, but transport carriers don't like transporting wine for consumers or one-off shipments. The carriers that will ship wine and alcohol are happy to ship these products for retail and online stores as regular senders like these know how to pack products for success. Strong sturdy cartons with the divider inserts should be used to stop the bottles from knocking against each other and are packaged firmly inside the carton. Do note that the transport providers generally do not cover you against broken glass.

Long items: Called 'lengths' in the industry, these can be hard to get right. Fishing rods, curtain rails, metal tunnels or anything over 1.2 m in length need some extra attention. They do not fit on a standard pallet base which then leaves them open to falling between pallets in transit, meaning they could be bent or crushed. These long items can also get caught or stuck in the conveyor belt bends in transport depots, stopping their operation and potentially damaging your product.

Thick cardboard tubes can be purchased and then cut to the desired length to protect these longer items. PVC pipes can also be used for these types of items. If you have a carpet layer or shop close by, they are often willing to give you the insert tube the carpet comes to them in, which is a great cheap solution. Use end caps to ensure your product doesn't slide out of the cardboard and PVC tubes in transit.

Odd-shaped items: What you need to remember is you will be charged for the whole space the item takes up on the truck, from the widest, deepest, highest point. It is not averaged out. As discussed in Chapter Three, pyramid-shaped items are going to be charged as a square or rectangle. Securely packing them into a carton with internal support is the best option.

Round-shaped items: Again, you're going to be charged as if it's a square. Take up the space and pack the item with as much internal support needed to ensure an on-time, intact delivery.

Musical instruments: Instruments come in a range of shapes and sizes. They need to be packed into a hard road case and a carton. As musical instruments can be valuable, the carton is as much for security as protection.

Surf, snow or wake boards: These need to have their fins removed, foam inserts or bubble wrap for internal protection then in a board carton. A padded travel bag alone is not enough in a shipping environment.

Furniture: If you're shipping assembled furniture, you need a furniture removalist company. Flat packed, ready to be assembled furniture can be shipped in new sturdy cartons with internal protection with carriers. Small side tables and chairs should be suitable for most carriers if in cartons under 20 kg.

Packaging correctly is vital to your online business's reputation and success. It's important you source and use new sturdy cartons. Do not re-use flimsy cartons and boxes, if possible.

If your items are on the heavier side, it's worth inserting corner triangle supports for added strength. We need the carton to be able to sustain and absorb some shock in transit. Getting a knock while in transit cannot be completely avoided but packing well means your goods still arrive on time and intact.

When in discussion with your supplier, much of the above can be done in the factory prior to importing the goods. A small extra cost for peace of mind, brand integrity and happy buyers is worth it.

ENSURING MINIMAL DAMAGE

One of our customers, Becca, was importing heavy vintage lockers for clothes from overseas (between

20 kg to 30 kg in deadweight), and sometimes the flat packs would be accidentally dropped by courier drivers and the corners of her products would be damaged upon arrival at her customer.

We discussed with her the option to use corner supports inside the cartons to protect the product should a flat pack be dropped in transit. She discussed this with her supplier and since implementing the corner supports inside the flat packs, she has had minimal to no issues with lockers being damaged in transit.

Moral of the story: Talk through your specific packing requirements with your supply network. Reputable shipping companies will know how best to manage your products.

TOP TIP: COVER IT UP

If you sell high-end, valuable or in-demand products, do not send the product in the flash product box advertising what is inside the box. It is best to hide the products from prying eyes to avoid theft during transit. You can place your flash product box inside a plain external brown or white shipping carton if required. This way, only the plain outer carton is seen by all.

Packaging solutions

Packaging suppliers have a range of products available to ensure you have everything you require for your items to be packed with enough protection to withstand shipping. Heavier items need new sturdy cartons with internal packaging like foam or peanut shells or biodegradable peanuts. Bubble-wrapping also provides a buffer between the outer carton and the internal goods.

We've heard sellers say, 'The extra packaging just adds to our costs'. Yes, it does, but let's talk about what you're protecting. It's more than the actual product. You are also protecting:

- Your brand

- Your business reputation

- Your credibility

Think about your packaging as an investment rather than an expense. Your goods making it to your customers on time and intact is what's getting you great online reviews and feedback. It's your lifeblood and future sales.

What it's saving you is:

- Your time in not having to deal with damaged product or reship replacement items

- Loss of margin due to damages
- Brand reputation

Keeping it lean and green

Brand damage can be caused to many companies these days as consumers are insisting we have an environmental conscience and do our part by reducing plastics and minimising landfill rubbish. For decades, the wasteful use of plastic packaging has contributed mountains of waste in landfill, giving off harmful gases into our atmosphere as well as polluting our oceans. Scientists warn us about global warming, and as business owners we need to reduce the amount of waste we create. Remember: recycle, re-use, reduce.

Internal packaging has historically been the hardest to replace with a sustainable, biodegradable bubble wrap, filler packing nuts and foam inserts. This has changed. Using products like 'wood wool' mushroom mycelium is an alternative to plastics and foams, or Oxo-B Eco Bubble is completely biodegradable. Packing tape can be biodegradable too. Some of your internal packaging products can be produced in-house using a cardboard recycling machine. Plain cardboard boxes and paper will always be biodegradable and a great option and will at least in part be made from recycled paper. You can also consider using a biodegradable shrink-wrap for your pallet shipments.

When designing your packaging, consider how the packaging can be repurposed by the receiver. For instance, could you create an incentive programme that would encourage the receiver to return the packaging to be re-used?

There is a difference between home compostable and commercial compostable. If the products you're looking into state they are biodegradable, they should then break down and return to the earth within six months. Some products are compostable but only in the home composter, which is ideal because it's not going to landfill, but not everyone you ship to will have a home composter.

TOP TIP

We recommend Hero Packaging (https:// heropackaging.com.au). These guys have a great range of completely biodegradable satchels and bubble-wrapped lined satchels that are zero waste. All profits go to the Rural Fire Service. Investing in environmentally friendly and biodegradable packaging is not only good for the planet but for your brand as well. It is a great marketing tool that many buyers happily will pay a little more for.

Summary of key points

In this chapter, we learned:

- The importance of choosing products that are easy to ship and why

- The different packaging solutions in the marketplace and why good packaging matters

- The lean and green packaging solutions available

SIX
Let's Get Techie

In this chapter, we discuss:

- Website platforms for eCommerce and recommendations

- Statistics on the best platforms and usage by merchants

- The benefits of using time-saving apps

- Technology used by carriers

- Shipping accountability through technology

Website platforms for eCommerce

In our fourteen-plus years as courier aggregators, we've invested serious time and money in developing and perfecting shipping technology solutions for eCommerce. When merchants evaluate eCommerce platforms, most look at how feature rich, cheap or expensive a platform is and its usability. These are all great things to take into account, but we look at it from a different angle altogether – shipping. It's one of the most important things to get right if you want to scale quickly in eCommerce. When your business starts ramping (and this can happen overnight if you're doing things right), you don't want to be behind and unable to get goods shipped out easily and efficiently.

Also consider looking at:

- **Hosting**: Server/hosting configuration is one of the biggest roadblocks when self-hosting your eCommerce solution. If you have developers that can help, great; if not, look for a platform that hosts your site for you.

- **Shipping APIs**: Does the platform provide an easy to digest API for developers to integrate with? If not, you may be stuck with no third-party apps/plugins or minimal choices to streamline your shipping.

- **Support**: Can you get quick and easy support with a human? Test this by logging two or three tickets over a week to see what the response times are or if they point you to self-help solutions.

- **App/plugin store:** Is there an easy one-stop location to access apps or plugins to help your workflow and save money and time? Are there lots of choices? If there are not, this most likely means it's a new platform, has no shipping APIs available or it's too difficult to integrate with.

What is an API?

An API – Application Programming Interface – is a gateway that allows software to talk to other software and manages how that conversation takes place. It allows a developer to write code to one piece of software that can then carry out certain actions without a developer having to write that software from scratch.

We recommend two eCommerce platforms in particular, for the following reasons:

Shopify

No server/hosting hassles: A Shopify store does away with the expense and pain of a self-hosted solution, just 'register', choose your apps and your theme and you're pretty much on your way. If you know a little about technology, you can even set up the webstore yourself (without the need for a web developer).

Easy to develop for: Shopify apps run on the web servers of the third-party developers who make them, so there are no surprises that can cause unexpected errors. Many other self-hosted eCommerce solutions add a layer of headaches – the merchant has to ensure that the web server specs are adequate and not causing problems.

Easy to support: It's easy for customers to get help, even with just the default Shopify support tools. It has simple and powerful integration and provides easy-to-use integration specs (API) that allow apps to extend store functionality, while keeping an eye on security (a bit like a Facebook app, you choose what the Shopify app has access to).

Plays nice with others: With some platforms, adding a new app or plugin can bring everything to a screaming halt. Shopify keeps everyone away from the parts that keep your site going, letting apps add functionality rather than destroy it. This means less support time and cost for app developers and merchants.

Easy to find an app: Shopify's App Store is laid out in a way that makes it easy to find the app you need, and to get your own apps found.

From our perspective, Shopify is one of the best platforms for merchants and an easy platform to develop shipping solutions for. If you're a merchant starting out or you're trading currently but looking to change platforms, we would highly recommend Shopify to help grow your online business and scale quickly.

WooCommerce

The other cart that we recommend is WooCommerce for WordPress. Similar to Shopify it has most of the same benefits for merchants (although you have to host the platform yourself). It is, however, flexible in the solutions you can develop (and not quite as rigid as Shopify).

Shopify and WooCommerce for WordPress are both mature and popular solutions in the marketplace (owning 50%+ share of the eCommerce technology space in Australia). As per the churn rates provided via Builtwith.com,[15] you can see a definite shift worldwide from other major platforms to these two over a number of years.

With some of their newer competitors (not listed), there is often a vast difference in the availability of eCommerce options (from a merchant's perspective and a developer's).

We love both these platforms and recommend them.

---

15 Builtwith.com

Statistics on the best platforms and usage by merchants

Churn rate* comparisons (global figures, January 2011 to August 2020)[16]

Shopify vs Magento	
Shopify to Magento	1,598
Magento to Shopify	16,672
Magento vs WooCommerce	
WooCommerce to Magento	2,391
Magento to WooCommerce	19,209
Magento vs BigCommerce	
BigCommerce to Magento	662
Magento to BigCommerce	1,771
Shopify vs BigCommerce	
Shopify to BigCommerce	1,854
BigCommerce to Shopify	5,604
WooCommerce vs BigCommerce	
WooCommerce to BigCommerce	787
BigCommerce to WooCommerce	2,991
Shopify vs WooCommerce	
Shopify to WooCommerce	23,087
WooCommerce to Shopify	23,730

*Churn rate means users that move from one solution to another.

NB These comparisons don't include 'Enterprise' versions of Shopify or Magento (those numbers are minimal compared to the standard platforms above).

Stats are based on the merchant being on the first cart and ending up on the second cart eventually (though possibly not directly).

Information is correct as at August 2020

---

16   BuiltWith.com

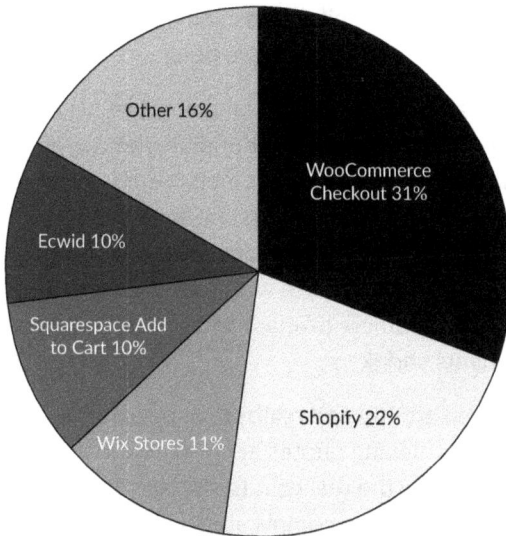

Distribution for websites using eCommerce technologies in Australia (January 2011–August 2020) [17]

WHEN FREE SHIPPING ENDS UP COSTING YOU

Jim ran a boutique beer business and decided to go online to increase sales. He noticed an advertisement for a free website platform and hired a website designer for a couple of thousand dollars to make his site look professional.

As he got close to going live, he noticed there weren't many options for shipping through the platform and he settled on offering free shipping Australia-wide. He worked out it would cost him around $30 to ship a case

---

17   BuiltWith.com

of beer to most capital cities and added this cost onto the sell price for his boutique beer.

Within a couple of months of going live, his sales were going through the roof, but upon reviewing his orders, he noticed 30% of his customers were in regional Australia. His shipping costs for these areas were more like $60 per case, making him little to no profit. This is a common occurrence with free shipping offers – regional customers take advantage and the margins for merchants shrink.

Jim asked around and realised he needed to either offer real-time shipping quotes at checkout on his site for buyers to pay the real cost to ship to their destination, or he had to set up complicated shipping rules establishing zones to offer dearer prices to regional and remote areas. This was all great, but the free site didn't provide the right solutions for shipping in their admin and there weren't any third-party apps available in Australia that could do what he needed.

Jim researched some more and found another eCommerce platform that could provide all these solutions for his webstore. Another couple of months and many thousands of dollars later, Jim was finally on track and had automated his whole logistics in the process.

The moral of the story: It pays to spend time to research as early as possible in your business journey the best solution from a shipping perspective as this can be a real bottleneck for you as you grow.

Time-saving apps

Anyone who has used shipping apps knows they can't do without them. As your sales grow, higher volumes of orders need to be shipped. In this day and age, you can't afford to be entering order information manually to generate shipping bookings and shipping labels. More importantly, you don't need to – there are many solutions that can streamline or even automate these processes. Most of these work via an API that is provided by your carrier or shipping provider.

How many shipping apps and solutions are available for you to use depends on which eCommerce platform you're using.

These are some of the time-saving benefits of using a shipping app when completing bookings for shipping (fulfilling orders):

• There is no need to manually re-enter your customer's name, phone number, delivery address, email address into the shipping platform.

• There is no need to manually re-enter the product(s) weight and dimensions of item(s) from the customer's order into the shipping platform.

• It generates real-time shipping quotes for you to choose from.

- It provides bulk fulfilment options – you can choose a range of orders to fulfil at once.

- It provides auto-fulfilment options allowing you to set some fulfilment rules around when orders can be automatically fulfilled.

- It returns PDF shipping labels to your store automatically once orders are fulfilled.

- It updates tracking numbers in your webstore admin automatically upon fulfilment.

Shipping apps can save up to 95% of your time when fulfilling orders. If you're a large-scale operation, imagine the cost savings this can bring to your bottom line.

Example:

Weekly hours   Hourly rate
to fulfil orders   for staff member

$$15 \times 95\% \ = \ 14.25 \times \$\,30.00 \times 52 \text{ weeks}$$

$$= \ \$\,22{,}230 \text{ (per year savings)}$$

Give it a go yourself:

Weekly hours   Hourly rate
to fulfil orders   for staff member

_____ × 95% = ____ × $____ per hour × 52 weeks

= $_____ (per year savings)

Added value benefits of shipping apps: Apart from saving you time in the logistics part of your business, a shipping app can also add value to your buyers in the following ways:

- Offer real-time shipping quotes at checkout.

- Present flat rate or free shipping rates at checkout.

- Establish shipping rules or zones via a stock-keeping unit (SKU), postcode ranges, countries, cart value, etc which enable you to present a custom shipping rate to buyers at checkout.

- Enable packages to be saved for quick use when fulfilling orders.

- Offer smart packing real-time algorithms which can combine multiple products in the cart into one condensed shipping package to save on shipping costs and shipping labels.

- Generate PDF shipping labels to print.

- Generate picking slips.

- Provide merchant with warnings of order or shipping issues.

- Automatically update receiver of goods with a tracking number or link to allow them to track the order themselves.

TIME IS MONEY

Mal owns and operates a small business. He works ten-hour days manufacturing his products, shipping out orders and, when he finds the time, doing the books. He did this for a number of years and with the business growing, he found he didn't have the time to do it all. Something had to change, particularly with the time-consuming area of shipping. It could take up to two hours per day to enter orders into the shipping platform's software, calculate shipping costs and generate shipping labels.

After discussing the issue with us, we provided a shipping app he could use to streamline this whole process with just a few clicks of a mouse. He managed to save 90% of his time involved in arranging shipping for orders by using our shipping app on his website. It meant a cost saving in his time of around $20,000 per year; more importantly, he gained back around nine hours per week, some of which he chose to spend with his family.

The moral of the story: Finding smart technology solutions can save you time and money.

Technology used by carriers

As mentioned in Chapter Two ('Courier reviews'), a number of Australian carriers have been purchased by overseas carriers in the past few years. The buyouts provided the Australian carriers with major funds to improve their businesses. These carriers were struggling to make improvements in their businesses prior to the buyouts, but since then nearly all have invested heavily in the following areas.

Depot improvements

With the ever-increasing demand for eCommerce deliveries, carriers and Australia Post have been busy building new larger depots in Australia to handle the volume. TNT, for example, built a new depot in Melbourne that could handle a reported 18,500 parcels per hour (an increase of 60% on previous capabilities);[18] new Super Hub depots in Sydney and Brisbane have also been built.

Australia Post has built a new $200 million depot in Redbank near Brisbane which can handle 700,000 parcels per day.[19] This is the largest parcel facility in the southern hemisphere.

---

18 TNT Australia, 'The world's largest TNT logistics "super hub" for Melbourne' [press release] (TNT Australia, 2014), www.tnt.com/express/en_au/data/news2010/press_release_tullamarine.html, accessed 28 January 2021; TNT, 'TNT Australia completes east coast super hub network' [press release] (TNT 2015), www.tnt.com/express/en_au/site/press/releases/east-coast-super-hub.html, accessed 28 January 2021

19 Goodman, 'Goodman commences development of the largest parcel facility and delivery centre in the southern hemisphere for Australia Post, to cater for growth in online sales' (Goodman, September 2018), https://au.goodman.com/who-we-are/media-centre/news/goodman-commences-development-of-parcel-facility-and-delivery-centre-for-australia-post

Dimensioner machinery

As discussed in Chapter Three, this is another big push for all carriers. This machinery recoups missed revenue due to under-declared weight and dimensions in bookings. Although the machines can be costly to install initially, over the long term they more than pay for themselves and bring in important revenues to the transport company's bottom line.

Sortation systems

These are the lifeblood of parcel transport depots. With huge volumes of parcels and products being shipped in eCommerce, the ability of humans to manually check and sort these items correctly at a high rate is not possible or feasible. As long as the drivers unload the products onto the conveyor belts with the shipping label facing up on the package, the products can be sorted correctly through the depot via the scanners on the conveyor belts and travel down the correct chute into the correct trailer or truck for delivery.

Some carriers may not have fully automated sortation systems or only some of their depots may have these available. It all comes down to the level of investment possible and number of depots they have nationally as the technology is not cheap.

Australia Post Redbank sortation system

Driver routing

This is a big-ticket item for all carriers. Although slow to be established in Australia, this software is key in providing efficiency. Instead of drivers planning their own route for the day with pick-ups and deliveries of consignments, this software will provide the driver via GPS with the most efficient route to take. Even if jobs are cancelled or changed throughout the day, the software updates in real time and reroutes the drivers along a new efficient path.

Driver routing monitors a driver's progress throughout the day ensuring they stick to the given route and timetable. The software knows how long a driver should take along their route based on historical data and real-time traffic updates.

Online portals

Some investment has been made in online quoting, booking and tracking systems by most of the transport companies. The nature of the transport industry is that carriers are primarily focused on providing efficient and timely transportation services. Most of their investment is used in achieving this goal.

Time-saving apps and solutions for eCommerce are usually provided by third parties and courier aggregators. Either way, the transport companies benefit and it's a win-win for all.

How technology enhances accountability

Tracking of goods is essential in eCommerce. When you can track a shipment, it provides peace of mind for the merchant as well as assurance and transparency for the buyer receiving the goods. You present yourself as a reliable brand. If you're selling on eBay, it assures eBay you've shipped the goods which is important (particularly for eBay Plus sellers as you need to meet despatch deadlines).

If you're using a provider that doesn't have tracking – change now.

Tracking can prove your shipment:

- Has been collected from you – which is helpful in insurance claims

- Is in transit – assuring the receiver the shipment is on the way

- Is heading in the right direction – while there are rare occasions when your shipment is not on track and has been misdirected to the wrong destination, tracking can help detect this earlier

- Has been damaged – a damaged scan is possible in some cases

- Has been delivered

- Has been delivered in the correct timeframe

There are some situations where tracking may not be possible:

- The barcode on the shipping label is damaged or covered and the transport company scanners cannot read the barcode.

- The barcode on the shipping label is faint or ineligible due to printer ink/toner issues when the label was printed.

- The shipping label has come off the package.

- A postal service is used that doesn't include tracking.

- The delivery is to a remote area where the end agent or carrier doesn't use scanners.

Do not be fooled into paying for tracking. There is no reason for any provider to charge you for the privilege of being able to track your shipments. Tracking is standard when the shipping label is provided to you with the barcode included on the label.

Real-time tracking apps

There are many apps available now that can update your eCommerce platform, eBay, etc with the tracking number in real time. This saves you spending time obtaining the tracking number and manually entering it into your system. These apps can also help automatically fire off an email/SMS to the receiver with the details to track the goods themselves. This service may come at a small cost, and we highly recommend taking advantage of it. When the receivers can track the shipment themselves or receive tracking updates, it provides them with assurance and stops them contacting you – wasting your staff's time and effort providing the update for them. It's not unheard of for some customers to continually contact a merchant asking for the delivery date or whereabouts of their order.

SAY YES TO TRACKING THE DRESS

Mary ran an online bridal gown business, and express delivery was important for Mary and her brand. Brides and their bridesmaids would sometimes place late orders, leaving Mary with minimal time to get the dresses made and shipped. She would receive phone calls from her customers asking for shipping updates on the whereabouts of their dress – this occurred on over 50% of orders.

Mary realised this had to change as much of her time was spent providing customer service for shipping rather than on new sales. She found a shipping service that offered a tracking number and link that was digitally sent to the receiver as soon as the order was fulfilled by Mary. The brides and bridesmaids could track the order themselves online. Incoming customer service calls reduced by 70% for Mary, allowing her to get back to making more sales and dressmaking.

The moral of the story: Providing your customers with tracking information can save you time and hassle.

Which carriers provide the best tracking experience

The larger courier and freight companies generally have better tracking systems. This comes down to the amount of money they can invest in their IT and infrastructure. They also have larger depot networks nationally, meaning that in most cases the goods stay within their own network and there is minimal reliance on onforwarding agents or other carrier networks to provide the data and scan the shipments for them (particularly in country areas of Australia).

125

Summary of key points

In this chapter, we learned:

- Our tips for choosing a website platform and shopping cart for eCommerce
- Why time-saving shipping apps are beneficial
- The main technology improvements that enable transport providers to efficiently and productively deliver products
- The role of tracking and its importance for maintaining buyer trust in a brand

SEVEN

Ready To Ship

In this chapter, we discuss:

- Shipping address and potential issues
- Shipping labels
- Third-party logistics (3PL)
- Dropshipping pros and cons

Shipping address and potential issues

Despatching address

You've got the right products for easy shipping and you're all packed and ready to ship, but there are a few more things of which you need to be aware.

When selecting the despatch address for your business, you need to know you will receive a regular and reliable service. Many fringe suburbs of metropolitan capital cities pose an issue as some are only serviced two or three days a week or are only serviced early in the morning. This is fine as long as you know, you've advised your buyer and the driver collects on the day. Avoid despatching from a gated community or an apartment block, if possible. As discussed previously, the drivers are only allocated a small time-window for each pick-up and or delivery. Parking and waiting to be buzzed in can be very time consuming for the drivers – and they may find it's all too hard, which could then result in you not receiving the service you require for your business. Often, there is nowhere safe you can leave the goods for the driver (an 'unattended pick-up') in these types of locations.

Remote areas mostly have limited service and are often serviced by an agent on behalf of the booked carrier. Usually, this causes a minimum of one business day delay and the tracking is not visible until the goods arrive at the main carrier's depot. This is less than ideal, especially if you're an eBay seller where the scanning is vital to your eBay agreement.

Pick-up issues

On-time pick-ups are imperative to the success of your online store. One way of ensuring this is having goods going out with each of your carriers on a daily basis. You arrange a pick-up time slot that is suitable to both you and the carrier. This doesn't work if you don't require a daily pick-up for each of your carriers. This can be problematic and one of the biggest issues for start-up online stores.

Online buyers want to be able to see their goods tracking in transit as you've advised them. eBay Plus members are required to provide eBay with the tracking number so they can monitor your sales are despatched on time. They will penalise you if your pick-ups are unreliable and inconsistent.

One way to ensure you receive a reliable service is to use a 3PL warehouse that can store, pick and pack your products and despatch them on your behalf.

OUT OF SIGHT, OUT OF MIND

We had a long-term customer who shipped from his home address in the Sydney metro area. After many years, he decided to move to a small town along the coast and moved his whole operation overnight. He booked his first shipments with us from the new address and the following day we received a phone call from him asking why the couriers hadn't collected his goods. We checked the new address and no courier company picked up from the address at all.

The address was located 5 km outside of a small regional town and wasn't serviced by any of our couriers, even the large companies. Dropping goods off at a post office in town wasn't an option either because his products were too large to send with Australia Post. His business suffered overnight as he couldn't despatch any orders, and he had to shut down his operation for a short period.

We assisted by getting his products into a 3PL warehouse in Sydney with one of our partners which actually was a blessing in disguise, as he went on to bigger and better things when he removed the bottleneck of despatch from his operation.

The moral of the story: Always check if an address can be serviced by carriers before moving house!

Develop relationships with your courier drivers

Any online business owner will tell you how important it is to their business that their delivery partners collect and scan their shipments on time, every time.

There can be many occurrences in the driver's day that may cause them to be delayed. Traffic and weather conditions, breakdown, road works, accidents, illness, acts of God and fatigue can all have an impact on the drivers. We get it can be frustrating, but the drivers are doing their best.

On the odd day they are running late or miss you altogether, instead of getting upset at the driver for inconveniencing you, try helping them load the vehicle or have a short chat about their day; be grateful they made the extra effort and got your orders on their way to your buyers. Understand that it isn't an easy job, and it is usually thankless. Some courier drivers work on a franchise owned business model, which means rather than being an employee of the courier company they are their own business owner. Like any business owner, some are better than others.

Your business relies on you getting the goods despatched as soon as possible. Make friends with your pick-up drivers so when they are really running behind, they'll make an extra effort to collect from you.

Shipping labels

Going back twenty to thirty years, shipping labels as they are today were non-existent. Carriers would provide a manual consignment note which was completed by pen. A multiple item consignment was tracked as a whole consignment rather than tracking per item as it is today.

When we were flirting with the idea of launching Australia's first online courier service over fourteen years ago, PDFs were only just becoming the norm for documents and internet transfers and emails. We were struggling with how to get the consignment notes to the sender of goods and then match the consignment note to the booking they would make online (this was going to be a manual and time-consuming process for the sender). PDF technology allowed us to generate barcoded consignment label(s) in real time, which could be emailed to the sender instantly when the booking was made on our website. With this issue resolved, Smart Send was born.

Some important factors to remember when using shipping labels:

- Apart from the shipping delivery address, the barcode on the label is just as important. Do not cover the barcode in any way (even with clear packaging tape) as the carrier's scanners may not be able to read the barcode and tracking of the item cannot occur.

- Ensure you regularly check the toner/ink in your printer, so the barcode and delivery address are readable by the carrier and their systems.

- If possible, use two labels on the package sent (in case one comes off in transit or is ripped). This will avoid lengthy delays or loss of your consignment.

- Otherwise, you should write the consignment number on the package also in case the label comes off in transit. This way the carrier can at least look up the consignment number in their system and generate a new label and get the goods delivered (please note, some carriers will charge you for this).

Important information on the labels

Apart from the delivery address and barcode already mentioned, the label also contains other vital information including:

- Pick-up address – important for carriers should the goods need to be returned to sender for any reason

- Sender and receiver phone numbers – important for carriers if they need to contact either the sender or receiver due to a delivery issue

- Number of items in the shipment – important should items from the consignment go missing in transit

- Total weight of shipment or individual weight of items in shipment – important for drivers and operations staff when sorting or lifting/loading the products into vehicles

- Total cubic volume

- Sortation codes – used by automated sortation machinery on conveyor belts in transport depots (or should manual sortation be required)

- Service type – informs operations staff and drivers of the type of service chosen for delivery

- Special instructions – informs operations staff and drivers of any special delivery or handling instructions

- Sender's reference – an invoice number/purchase order for the order

- Consignment number – used to differentiate the consignment from others in the carrier's system

- Carrier name – most carrier labels are different from one another but in case they're not, this informs the carrier that the consignment is to be transported by a certain carrier

What type of label formats are there?

The two most popular label formats are:

- A4

- 6 inch × 4 inch (also known as thermal label)

If you're just starting out in eCommerce or are still a low volume sender, the A4 format is fine and you can simply print onto an A4 sheet of paper and stick that to the package sent. You can buy A4 labels, but they are expensive.

Be sure to only use a laser printer and not a bubblejet or inkjet printer (as the ink in these two printer types will run if the label gets wet in transit and you will have delivery or loss issues).

If you are starting to send decent volumes, you should look at using a thermal label printer which will print the 6 inch × 4 inch label format. For these printers, you use a roll of labels that are adhesive and will easily peel off and adhere to the parcel. There are many brands of thermal label printers, with Zebra or Dymo being two popular printers. If you're looking for value for money, we recommend the **Dymo Label-writer 4XL printer**.

Manifests

As well as the consignment label you stick to the goods, most carriers will require you to provide a manifest for the day's despatching even if only shipping one item. The manifest includes a breakdown of the consignments sent and most of the information that appears on the consignment label. There is a space to sign your name and date the manifest, and the pick-up driver keeps this manifest for their internal purposes. Most online carrier and courier aggregator systems will produce the manifest for you automatically to print off and provide to the driver.

Third-party logistics (3PL) as a solution

Most businesses ship from their own warehouse (or from home for smaller entities or start-ups). This makes sense when starting out as it helps to have good control over your logistics and costs. As you grow, however, it comes with such long-term setbacks as:

- High expenses when running a warehouse (ie lease, electricity, staff wages, legals, insurance, etc)

- Your home eventually running out of room when product volumes increase over time

- Lost opportunity cost due to focusing on getting orders out the door, rather than focusing on the big picture (ie efficient shipping strategy, sales and growing your business)

3PL is generally a term used for specialised warehouses that can store, pick and pack, and ship your product sales orders on your behalf. You take the customer order and the 3PL service gets your product to your customer (this is different to dropshipping).

Using a 3PL service most likely comes at a certain time in your business lifecycle, usually when you're starting to scale up (we find when you're shipping fifteen-plus orders per day as a general rule). Until recently most 3PL services only catered to large volume customers, but these days start-ups can also access these services.

Product profile does come into the equation, though. Generally, if you're selling low-cost products (less than $20), you may struggle to be able to afford the storage and pick and pack costs associated with this type of service. Be aware that 3PL services don't include shipping unless you request it, so factor in the shipping costs you will need to have the orders delivered to your customers also (you can usually specify your own carrier or account to be used with a 3PL service). The key is to turn over (sell) your products as quickly as possible, as you will pay weekly costs for storage that will eat into your margins over time if the products are just sitting on a shelf for long periods.

The beauty of 3PL is it removes the majority of cost, time and effort of logistics from your business, leaving all that to the 3PL provider and allowing you to focus on opportunities for more sales, partnerships and growing your business. They can also handle returns for you should the need arise, so ask for the costs associated with this service before you start.

With the advent of new technological solutions, you can fulfil orders from your eCommerce platform directly with a 3PL provider. This process can even be automated, if you prefer, which saves you lots of time in your business. Imagine clicking the fulfil button on your platform and the order is done, dusted and shipped with your 3PL provider.

Before deciding on a 3PL provider, it is important to consider the potential advantages and disadvantages of using such a service.

Advantages

- 3PL providers are specialists in logistics and fulfilment.

- Using a 3PL provider removes high costs associated with fulfilment from your business.

- Using a 3PL provider allows you to scale quickly.

- Your saved funds can go toward revenue generating activities.

- Using a 3PL provider saves you time and effort in your business which means less stress.

Disadvantages

- 3PL services are not available to every business due to cost.

- 3PL providers usually won't deal with your customers if issues arise with an order / shipment.

- There are cut-off times to get orders out same day.

- You need to ensure that your 3PL provider can integrate and work seamlessly with your eCommerce platform.

According to a report published by Allied Market Research, the global 3PL market was pegged at $1,027.71 billion in 2019 and is anticipated to reach

$1,789.94 billion by 2027, growing at a CAGR of 7.1% from 2020 to 2027.[20]

Dropshipping

Dropshipping is different to 3PL as with dropshipping you don't need to own or hold the stock or products yourself. You don't need to have them manufactured or even pay for them until you sell the product. You simply negotiate with dropshipping manufacturers or suppliers for products you would like to sell. When you sell these via your eCommerce platform, the order information is provided to the dropshipper you're working with, and they will ship the goods to your customer for you on your behalf.

Like with 3PL, there are potential advantages and disadvantages to consider with dropshipping.

Advantages

• You don't need large upfront investment on inventory.

---

20 A Sonpimple, 'Third-party Logistics (3PL) Market by Mode of Transportation (Railways, Roadways, Waterways, and Airways), Service Type (Dedicated Contract Carriage (DCC), Domestic Transportation Management, International Transportation Management, Warehousing & Distribution, and Others) and Industry (Technological, Automotive, Retailing, Elements, Food & Groceries, Healthcare, and Others): Global opportunity analysis and industry forecast, 2020–2027' (Allied Market Research, 2020), www.alliedmarketresearch.com/3pl-market, accessed 29 January 2021

- It is easier to scale – the dropship partner ships products and does returns for you.

- You don't need a warehouse or staff to process and fulfil orders.

- It minimises the chances of large losses if you choose a bad product to sell as you only pay for the product once you sell the product.

- There are no managing stock levels or inbound shipments from the manufacturer.

- You can run your business from anywhere that has an internet connection.

- You can have a large range of products when starting out.

Disadvantages

- Other merchants could be selling the exact same product as you and using the same photos provided by the dropshipper (ie your products may not be unique). It's difficult to have your own brand when using a dropshipping model.

- Margins on sales are much lower than a traditional business model.

- Different suppliers could use different methods to communicate with your system (automated or manual). This could hinder tracking updates, shipping rates for buyers in your system or make it difficult to use one system to handle this process.

- Buyers can receive orders late, or if multiple item orders are from different suppliers, the items are received at different times rather than all at once. This is not a great experience for your buyer or your brand.

- You could sell products that aren't in stock or not available currently by your dropshipper. To avoid this, you should check if they have an auto-update method to inform you of stock levels.

There are technology solutions in the marketplace to handle some of these issues and streamline a drop-ship business model. It depends on how much control or brand strength you're after for your business and whether you would use this type of model.

Summary of key points

In this chapter, we learned:

- How to make it easy for drivers to collect and the importance of developing a good relationship with drivers

- Important facts about shipping labels

- Whether 3PL might be a good option

- What dropshipping is and whether it might be a good fit

EIGHT

Delivered On Time And Intact

In this chapter, we discuss:

- Common delivery issues

- Customer service standards

- Peak Christmas period shipping

- Acts of God

- COVID-19 and the carrier response

Common delivery issues

Many delivery issues are caused by not enough information on the label. For example: if your receiver is at a business address, the business name should always be included, even if the receiver is receiving personal items. If it's not included, the carrier may declare the address as incomplete, and charge you a redirection fee for a new label which includes the business name. There are good reasons for this. In industrial or commercial areas, the street number is extremely hard to find but the business name is easily seen by the driver. Including the business name will avoid unnecessary delays for all parties.

If you're an online shopper, consider what address you use on eBay, Google or Amazon to ensure it's a complete address and the driver is able to deliver easily the first time. If you live in a secure apartment building or a gated community, use a business address instead if possible. As a seller, if you have given an ATL for the consignment and the driver is unable to gain access to the address or contact your customer, the driver may leave the goods at the main door, and you generally have no recourse in these situations.

These situations are frustrating for everyone in the chain: the receiver, driver, depot. Everyone incurs additional costs, double handling – it's a no win for all parties involved.

As eCommerce grows year on year in Australia, the industry has risen to the challenge to provide solutions in situations where a delivery cannot be made to the door of the receiver. There can be many reasons why a door-to-door service is not possible:

- If the receiver is in a metro 'fringe' area, it may not be serviced.

- The receiver may live on a farm or Outback address.

- The receiver may have an address with dirt road access only.

- Residences with steep driveways can cause issues with heavy item deliveries.

- Some carriers will only service certain parts of a rural or regional town.

In these situations, Australia Post and StarTrack Express will deliver to the local post office for collection where possible.

As discussed earlier, all other carriers now have a collection network in place (see Chapter Three).

X-ray vision

Due to the strengthened government domestic aviation security measures, all express and air carriers in Australia must screen all items travelling via aircraft across Australia. Further information can be found at: www.homeaffairs.gov.au/about-us/our-portfolios/transport-security/air-cargo-and-aviation.

Mail and air cargo are screened through X-ray and explosive trace detection (ETD) machinery. It is important to consider if your products can be subjected to these forms of examination. If you are unsure, contact your express carrier and discuss further.

Customer service

We all want to give our customers the best possible customer service, but this can be difficult and time consuming once the goods leave your warehouse.

When selecting your delivery partners, you want to be assured you and your customer are going to receive the best possible customer service when things go wrong. This is transport – things will go wrong once in a while. Around five out of 100 shipments will have some sort of issue, and that's when using the best carriers in the marketplace.

Most carriers want you to lodge a query via their online portal and will provide around a four- to five-hour reply time at best, although most have an automated reply to let you know they have received the query initially. Some carriers say twenty-four to forty-eight hours is a reasonable response time. Depending on the time of year (peak periods or quiet periods), reply times to online queries or any query can take far longer. This can be extremely frustrating and time consuming especially when your customer is pushing you for answers.

Let's discuss why some of these delays occur. It's easier when you understand how transport companies operate in Australia. Not one transport company is able to service the whole of Australia alone, this includes Australia Post.

To deliver to the entire country, an agent network is in place to cover the more regional areas. Companies like Regional Freight Express is in effect a whole range of agents that come together under the banner to deliver into some rural and regional areas. At time of writing, major carriers such as TNT and Toll (and many more) pass their rural freight to the agent for delivery in the areas they cannot or do not cover themselves.

How does this affect your customer service experience? If you have a late delivery, lodge a query with the carrier, either online or over the phone, they will give you a query number. They lodge a query with the agent who will lodge a query with their agent. It's time consuming, and on top of that, there may be no scans once the goods are in the agent network as it passes from one agent to the next, and you'll have no visibility even using today's technology.

Some carriers have their customer service teams based offshore. Most have great English skills, but if not based in Australia, it can be difficult to get hold of them when it's urgent. In some cases, they cannot even connect you to an Australian-based supervisor if required.

It's important to note some key statistics about unhappy customers:[21]

- The average business never hears from 96% of its unhappy customers.

- Complainers are more likely than non-complainers to do business again with the company that upset them even if the problem is not resolved satisfactorily.

- 54%–70% of customers who register a complaint will do business again with the organization if the complaint is resolved. That figure goes up to a staggering 95% if the customer feels that the complaint was resolved quickly.

- A satisfied customer tells eight people, whereas a dissatisfied customer tells twenty-two.

- Acquiring a new customer can cost up to ten times as much as supporting an existing customer.

- Loyal customers generate higher profit margins than new customers. Studies indicate that a 5% improvement in customer retention can add anywhere from 25% to 85% to the bottom line.

- A 10% increase in customer retention adds up to 30% to customer value.

---

21 L Tatikonda, 'The hidden costs of customer dissatisfaction', *Management Accounting Quarterly* (2013), 14/3, 34–43, www.imanet.org/-/media/3624cb55dea84e3c8285bbb5b97fe4e4.ashx, accessed 28 January 2021

Available customer service technology

Most carriers now use cloud-based customer service platforms like Zendesk, Salesforce, etc to control and monitor their open customer service queries. These platforms should give you more options on how they keep you up to date (phone, chat, email or text) while you're on the move. Some of these systems can be integrated to your own customer service platform. It's worth asking your carriers the question.

When selecting your delivery partner, make sure you've asked these questions to be clear on time frames from first reply to completion. This way you'll know what the carrier key performance indicators (KPIs) are and know what to advise your own customers in return.

Personalised customer service for larger customers

If you're a regular sender spending over $250,000 per annum with your carrier, you should be in a position to request and have a contact team to help you sort your customer service needs. This should improve response times dramatically.

One option emerging in the marketplace is branded customer service. For a fee, the provider will answer and look after your customer service needs, answering as your business/brand to your customers.

For a small amount of your time training the provider's team (that will deal with your customers) about your business and how you operate, they will reply to your customer as if your customer were dealing directly with your business, so you can get on with your business doing what you do best.

The big bonus for you is reducing internal costs such as the hidden costs of employing customer service staff to deal with customer shipping queries. As your partnered support staff will look after more than one customer, there are significant labour cost savings for your business over the long term.

No matter what your size, when selecting your delivery partners, you need to ask all the right questions to be clear on what you can expect when delivery issues arise.

Last-minute Christmas shipping

Every year as we lead into Christmas, we warn people not to leave their shipping (and shopping) to the last minute. The carrier's systems get backed up and it's a recipe for disappointment. It's imperative you keep your customers informed of cut-off dates to ensure they receive their Christmas gifts on time and don't miss out. A header notification on your website or message in your eBay listing is sufficient.

A CHRISTMAS STORY

Christmas this particular year was late in the week (Thursday or Friday). As you would expect, the transport depots were working hard on clearing their operations as much as possible before the big day.

We received an enquiry from a grandmother based on the Sunshine Coast in Queensland about getting her gifts to her grandchildren on the Gold Coast. She wanted to know if she sent their presents on the 22 December would the goods arrive on the 24 December. We explained this was a big ask the week before Christmas with the backlogs and that it was highly unlikely – we could not guarantee the goods would arrive on time. She came back stating that it was only a two-and-a-half-hour drive and asked why it wasn't possible. We explained that unless she wanted to use a direct drive service (which is extremely expensive), the gifts needed to travel through three different depots and each depot meant a day's delay at this time of year. Still, she couldn't understand why the gifts would not arrive on time.

Eventually she asked if the depots opened on Christmas Day for last-minute deliveries. By this time, we were so perplexed we said, 'Maybe we can get the driver to dress up as Santa and deliver the gifts.' She was so excited by this and said, 'Really?' We then had to say, 'Sorry, no, the driver will be at home enjoying Christmas with his own family.'

The moral of the story: Flag up to your customers not to leave their important shopping and shipping to the last minute. Whether it be Christmas or any other important event during the year, encourage them to get in early and leave plenty of time for delays and human error. Remind your customers, the early bird catches the worm!

Acts of God

Sometimes things happen that are completely out of your control and the carrier's. We can think of several that stand out over recent times.

2010/11 Queensland floods

Not only did these floods impact Brisbane and surrounding areas, there were floods all the way up the Queensland coast. Areas of Brisbane were closed for several weeks as they were deemed too unstable for the vehicles to enter.

When we told one sender his goods couldn't be delivered, he rather sarcastically replied, 'I don't have to paddle to work.' The depot the goods were being sent from had flooded and the knock-on delay took weeks for the carrier to catch up on to get back to normal delivery standards.

In this situation, the trucks heading north to Bundaberg, Rockhampton, Mackay and through to Cairns could not get through because the highway was closed to heavy vehicles.

2019/20 Summer fire season

This fire season was devastating for many parts of Australia, in particular for the south coast of New South Wales. Our hearts go out to all those who lost loved ones, their homes or were affected in other ways.

As you can imagine, this delayed deliveries into all affected areas and, in some cases, essential food deliveries were unable to get into towns isolated by fire.

2020 COVID-19 lockdown

Throughout 2020, we were struggling with the COVID-19 pandemic. February to May would normally be a quiet time of the year for carriers spent reviewing the peak Christmas season from the previous year and planning for the coming peak season leading into Christmas. Staff are generally encouraged to take leave during this time.

COVID-19 changed transport operations dramatically due to social distancing, testing and other precautions required to keep this vital industry moving. To add to the pressure, the Victorian coronavirus outbreak in July/August of 2020 meant that at one point the Victorian Government asked all transport companies to reduce staffing numbers by 30%. The industry responded exceptionally, particularly because the industry saw unprecedented shipment volumes moving through their systems – some saying this period was bigger than the peak 2019 Christmas shipping season.

Carriers dealing with COVID-19

In *Carrying On*,[22] Smart Send's guide released during the peak of the COVID-19 outbreak in Australia, Steven Visic spoke with four of the major courier companies on how the coronavirus impacted their operations.

Simon Sproule, a Partner Manager at Fastway Aramex, said:

> It has been a double hit. On one side of the ledger, we are doing all we can to keep our couriers and our employees safe as well as our customers, with things like not accepting signatures and a lot of measures in the depots to make sure people aren't cross contaminating each other.

Mark McGinley, CEO at Couriers Please, said:

> I'm really proud of what we've been able to achieve over the COVID-19 period. Obviously, we've had to invoke our social distancing

---

22 Smart Send, *Carrying On* (Smart Send, 2020), https://shippingsmarter.com.au/carrying-on, accessed 28 January 2021

protocols and our BCP protocols, and it has
had an impact on the operation. We've had
to extend our sortation times into night shifts
and weekend shifts so as to allow less people
in the facility at any one time. We've also
had to stagger our depot times so there's less
franchisees in the depot at the same time. The
company has introduced contactless deliveries
and contactless pick-ups.

Ben Franzi, General Manager Parcel and Express
Services at Australia Post, StarTrack, said:

There's probably been three big impacts from
COVID-19. The first one is the dramatic rise in
B2C volume. You're seeing anywhere between
60 to 80% growth in B2C, which is impacting
the demand for products across all the
Australia Post and StarTrack networks.

The second big one has been the lack of
passenger flights flying in the country. With
QANTAS and Virgin grounded, there's very
few passenger flights and a big component of
(our) air network was using passenger flights.
We've brought on more freighters to get more
planes in the air to be able to cope with the
volume and upped our freighter fleet to try
to replace some of that passenger capacity we
were previously using.

Michelle McDowell, Managing Director at Allied Express, said:

> As a transport company, we knew early on that people would be relying on us. So, we did a lot of work to make sure that our people were safe. This included good social distancing and hygiene measures. We were temperature controlling people entering our facilities very early in the piece, both in the offices and the depots. All our deliveries, from very early on, were contactless. What we tried to do was set up very well at the beginning of the pandemic. And I think that stood us in good stead for actually moving through the weeks and months that came after that.

Summary of key points

In this chapter, we learned:

- How residential addresses are harder to deliver to for many reasons

- How customer service in transport is vital so it is important to choose a partner wisely

- To get Christmas orders out early and keep customers informed

- Acts of God are unfortunate, but when they do occur, it is in everyone's best interest to be patient and considerate of the impact on carriers and providers

- COVID-19 news from four of the big eCommerce carriers in Australia

In Conclusion

The ever-increasing growth of online shopping bodes well for any business already in the online space. If you're not online, what are you waiting for?

Key takeaways

Here are some key tips from each chapter for shipping successfully.

Chapter One: Here we covered why you need to become an online retailer, if you are not already. It's important to be sure you have a multi-channel model for your business. Don't get stuck selling on one platform or marketplace only; you may do OK, but you won't experience the full opportunities available to you and the exceptional growth potential for your business that multi-channel offers.

Chapter Two: We addressed aligning your brand with the right carrier. Research the industry and don't be scared to ask the hard questions. Two top tips are to align yourself with provider(s) that project the same standards as your business and use a variety of carriers to ship your products if possible – you'll get the best bang for your buck and a broader range of services to offer your customers.

Chapter Three: We covered the basics of shipping in Australia. Understanding these will give you a great grounding to ensure you save on shipping in many different areas. Our top tip would be to spend some time evaluating your product profile and assess how to ship easier, faster and at a lower cost by reviewing the shipping pricing and cubic charging sections.

Chapter Four: We considered how to avoid less than ideal surprise fees. Getting stung with surcharges or penalties due to an incorrect declaration or by misunderstanding your requirements can be costly. We recommend assessing any potential surcharges you could receive in transport and particularly whether any of your product line is classified as dangerous or hazardous goods.

Chapter Five: Here we got into packing for success. Over the years, we've come across many customers who have sourced the wrong products or not spent time researching how they could ship the goods easily or cost effectively before starting. If we could invent a time machine, we would help these customers *before* they placed the first order with their supplier and spend some time investigating all the avenues that would allow them to become successful shippers. It's such a key area of success when shipping: the right product and packaged correctly.

Chapter Six: We looked at the tech side of things. Two game changers here are to use both shipping apps and an eCommerce platform suitable for eCommerce. Without either, you will forever be working in the business and not on your business. Your ability to scale and become a high-growth success story will be limited and also unlikely.

Chapter Seven: We discussed being ready to ship and important considerations you should be aware of. The big-ticket item here is your pick-up address. This leads to many problems with either missed or late pick-ups. If you're at a point where you're sending decent volumes out each day, considering a 3PL solution is also a smart move in removing high fixed costs from your business and allowing you more time to work on your business and grow faster.

Chapter Eight: Common delivery issues were considered which are great to have in mind when dealing with your customers. The one less thought about (or considered aspect of shipping) that we shout from the rooftops regularly is customer service. Spend the time to find a provider that can become an experienced partner for your business, that will assist you during the ongoing shipping issues you will experience during your shipping journey. Your shipping success story depends on it.

We have helped thousands of customers succeed with shipping and we have a special yearning to help startup and small businesses succeed when shipping their goods. It's a passion we hold to this day to see a fledgling idea or product come to fruition and become a shipping success story. Similarly, we are passionate about assisting an existing business that is struggling with overwhelming shipping problems, helping it come out the other side stronger and better than before.

We hope you have gained a wealth of knowledge and information to aid you in your shipping journey. It's a long one with ever bending twists and turns along the way but planning from the start will result in a smoother ride.

Smart Sender Scorecard

Our Smart Sender scorecard is a free test done online in less than 5 minutes:

https://smartsendertest.smartsend.com.au

It is designed to give you a powerful and important analysis of how well your business measures up against key areas of shipping success.

You will receive a Smart Sender score instantly & advice on how to improve your current scores (if required).

Glossary Of Industry Jargon

Common terms

ATL: Authority to leave. This means a delivery driver has been given authority by you to leave the goods at the delivery address and no signature is required.

Carrier: A transport company, courier, freight or bulk delivery service.

Consignment: A shipment of goods to one receiving address. This can consist of one item or multiple items.

Depot: A warehouse or shed used to sort, check, scan and ultimately deliver goods for a customer.

Duties (or customs duties): This is a tax imposed on goods when they are transported internationally. The government uses this duty to raise its revenues, safeguard domestic industries and regulate movement of goods.

Freight profile: What the goods sent look like, weight, cubic size, product type, packaging used, etc.

Interstate: Delivery of goods into a different state of Australia from the state they were sent.

Intrastate: Delivery of goods within the same state of Australia.

Linehaul: Usually a large truck that transports mixed customer products from one carrier depot to another (this could be a short local trip or interstate).

Pallet: A wooden structure with an approximate length and width of 117 cm × 117 cm long and an approximate height of 10 cm to 15 cm that can be placed at the base of or under heavy products to allow a forklift to easily load or unload the product from containers or trucks without damaging the base of the product with the forklift's tines.

Provider: This can mean a transport company, courier, freight carrier, Australia Post, aggregator or broker that assists a business with delivering their goods.

Signature on delivery/receipted delivery: If this service is chosen, it means the driver must obtain a signature from the receiver to effect delivery of the goods.

SME: This means a small to medium-sized enterprise.

Two-man service: This means a service where two staff members and a truck were sent to deliver the goods (usually used for heavier items).

YOY: This means year on year.

Carrier tracking scans

Each carrier's scans can be different. This guide will help you to understand what some of the main scans mean:

AGT	Agent
AMIN	Morning scans into a depot
AMOUT	Morning scan out of a depot
ATL	Authority to leave
DEL	Delivered
DIM	Dimensioner machine scans
DIMS	The good's dimensions
DIT	Damaged in transit

DMG	Damaged
ETA	Estimated time of arrival
ETD	Estimated time of delivery
Futile	Driver attempted collection/goods not available
LIB	Left in bay at depot
LID	Left in dock/left in depot
LIT	Lost in transit
LOD	Left on dock/left in depot
MHL	Manual handling
ONF	Onforwarded to agent
PMIN	Afternoon/evening scans into a depot
PMOUT	Afternoon/evening scans out of a depot
POD	Proof of delivery
RTS	Returned to sender

Main depot codes

ABX	Albury
ADL	Adelaide
BAL	Ballarat

BEN	Bendigo
BNE	Brisbane
CC	Central Coast
CRN	Cairns
DEV	Devonport
DUB	Dubbo
HOB	Hobart
LCN	Launceston
MEL	Melbourne
MKY	Mackay
NCL	Newcastle
OOL	Gold Coast
PER	Perth
ROK	Rockhampton
SYD	Sydney
SSC	Sunshine Coast
TMW	Tamworth
TVL	Townsville
TWB	Toowoomba

The Authors

Steven Visic – Director of Sales at Smart Send

Steven has had a twenty-eight-plus year career in the Australian transport industry in a variety of roles including customer service, operations, sales and management. He was lucky enough to bed his wares early on with Australia's most respected freight company, McPhee Transport, in the early 1990s, gaining invaluable knowledge and experience for his long career in transport.

In 2006, he and business partner and co-Director Chris Madden became the forerunners in the online courier industry and began Australia's first online courier service, Smart Send. Steven is acknowledged as a Shipping Expert by PayPal and Smart Send is a recommended shipping option by eBay Australia.

Chris Madden – Director of Operations at Smart Send

After a long, successful career in sales, Chris fell into the transport industry and loved it from the start. Over time, she was promoted from sales into managing positions. For the past fifteen years, Chris has run the operations side of Smart Send, a company she created with Steven.

Chris believes there are fundamental mistakes eCommerce businesses make from the start and is passionate about educating online businesses on how to maximise their deliveries by selecting the right last mile delivery partner(s).

You can read up on our shipping articles and information or contact us:

⊕ SmartSend.com.au

🔊 https://shippingsmarter.com.au

www.ingramcontent.com/pod-product-compliance
Lightning Source LLC
Chambersburg PA
CBHW071552200326
41519CB00021BB/6711